ROLLING IN CRYPTO

Prospering In The Uprise Of The Decentralised Economy

Herzig Ansel

Version 3.3, Print Format

Copyright © 2018. Herzig Ansel.

All rights reserved.

No part of this publication may be reproduced, distributed, or transmitted in any form or by any means, including photocopying, recording, or other electronic or mechanical methods, without the prior written permission of the publisher, except in the case of brief quotations embodied in critical reviews and certain other noncommercial uses permitted by copyright law.

For permission requests, contact author.

Acknowledgements

My deepest gratitude to my family who have fostered the creative environment and supported my basic needs unreservedly.

To my friends who have supported me mentally, believed in me, and kept me sane the whole time, thank you for pushing me and seeing me through this journey.

To the people who have read my work, thrown me ideas, given me all the critique and feedback whether it is in the execution, the writing, or the designs, you have helped shaped this book into what it is today.

I started writing this book as a personal goal – to create something of my own. At the end of the day, I realised that this was more than just me. It was the bits of contributions, from many different individuals, that helped transform this book into the final product.

Preface

It all started with an accidental foray into cryptocurrencies.

When I first started, I was overwhelmed with new concepts of blockchain technology and cryptocurrencies. My attempts to articulate and explain these concepts often fell short but my knowledge and understanding of this field gradually deepened.

Cryptocurrencies and distributed ledgers quickly became my reality and I found myself constantly reading whatever available resources and jotting down notes as I went along. These little pockets of notes became blog articles, which later grew into the many ideas incorporated in this book. Writing is my way of documenting my journey down the crypto rabbit hole.

Cryptocurrencies span across multiple disciplines from computer programming to finance and investing. However, the space has been littered with too much misinformation and inaccurate depictions that are largely perpetuated by mainstream media. The objective of this book is to cut out all the noises so that a layman can easily grasp the technical concepts and feel confident about investing in this new technological revolution.

I see cryptocurrencies manifesting in two forms. The first is a technological advancement whose success is contingent on its development and eventual adoption. This relates to the functional aspect of distributed ledger technologies (DLT), its impact on society, and how it changes the way people transact with one another.

Throughout the course of history, technology has shaped our way of life. From the invention of paper and the printing press, to mechanisation during the Industrial Revolution and the modern era of computers and the Internet, these technological groundbreakers come about once every few decades.

Cryptocurrency is the next paradigm.

The second notion of cryptocurrencies, which is also the focus of this book, is about them as an asset class that is traded, speculated, and manipulated — cryptoassets.

'Cryptoassets' is just one particular use case of DLT, where coins and tokens are a layer built on top of the technology and then traded. This tokenisation phenomenon has enabled various industries to innovate and create new revenue streams through tokens but it has also been misused by some companies who create tokens for the sake of jumping onto the crypto bandwagon.

As cryptocurrencies and DLT are relatively new, security lapses are frequent, scams are common, regulatory changes are unpredictable, and market volatility is wild. Hence, investments in cryptocurrency are very risky but it is this combination of uncertainties and risks that presents a valuable opportunity.

The first section of the book introduces some basic concepts about blockchain technology and distributed ledgers. It alludes the crypto investment journey to the wild and whimsical adventure in Wonderland, where most first-timers will be caught unprepared. For those who have read about cryptocurrencies or the technology underpinning them, this chapter should reinforce your existing knowledge of how blockchain works. It should also give an idea of their significance in society and why they are relevant to you.

The second part of the book dives into the crazy and unpredictable world of investing and trading in cryptocurrencies. You will be introduced to a qualitative approach of assessing cryptocurrencies so that you can curate your own mid to long-term crypto portfolio. Various strategies and tactics will also be covered so that you can optimise your capital, make strategic entries and exits, and minimise your risks.

The last part of the book explores the potential upsides and threats surrounding the crypto space. By looking critically at many of these issues, you will understand that cryptocurrency, like any other investments, has its own set of risks. Having a solid understanding of the fundamentals and a proper risk management strategy in place will help you invest safely and effectively.

More importantly, it is when you see the plausibility of a decentralised economy will you be confident about DLT and the future of cryptocurrencies. While reading the book, I would like to invite everyone to keep an open frame of mind, to entertain the possibilities, and to develop your own stance and criticisms.

There is no one who can be absolutely right in the cryptocurrency space now.

H. Ansel

> *"Play the market, and try not to be played by it."*
> — *Hansel.*

I: Down The Rabbit Hole – Crypto 101

Chapter 1
Wealth In The New Technology Revolution

Introduction to Blockchain and Distributed Ledger Technology — 3

Cryptocurrencies – A Use Case of DLT — 11

Cryptocurrencies – A New Technology Paradigm — 15

Cryptocurrency As An Investment — 20

Chapter 2
Getting Started On Cryptocurrencies

Buying Your First Cryptocurrency — 25

Buying and Selling Altcoins — 27

Storage of Cryptocurrencies — 30

II: Mad As A Hatter – Crypto Investing Essentials

Chapter 3
Investing Is About Active Risk Management

Determining Your Risk Profile — 34

Laying Down Your Ground Rules — 36

Generic Strategies for Cryptocurrency Investing — 38

Chapter 4
Building Your Personalised Crypto Portfolio

Evaluating The Fundamentals — 44

An Alternative Cryptocurrency Taxonomy — 51

The Myth Of Diversification — 57

Chapter 5
Thriving In The Wild Wild West

Investing-Specific Tactics — 59

Trading-Specific Tactics — 61
A Preview Of Technical Analysis — 66
Case Study: IOTA (MIOTA) — 69
Taking Profits And Reevaluating Trades — 71

Chapter 6
Market Forces And Human Behaviour
Playing In A 24/7 Global Market — 74
Hitching Alongside The Manipulators — 77
Understanding Market Psychology — 81

III: Through The Looking Glass – The Future Beholds

Chapter 7
Common Arguments Against Cryptocurrencies
The Promise of Decentralisation — 88
The Uncertainty of State Regulations — 91
The Possibility of a Speculative Bubble — 92
The Sustainability of Mining — 97
The Threat of Security Lapses — 101
The Speculation Fuelled by The Media — 106

Chapter 8
Looking Beyond Today's Noise And Speculation
Regulating Your Emotions — 110
Looking At Alternative Investments — 111
Cutting Down On Crypto-Obsession — 114
Distributed Ledgers: The Bridge Between Digital And Reality — 116
The Future of DLT — 120

I: Down The Rabbit Hole – Crypto 101

"Curiouser and curiouser!" cried Alice.

Chapter 1
Wealth In The New Technology Revolution
What is cryptocurrency? Why is it worth our time, and money?

Today, if you were to initiate a conversation about "cryptocurrency", you will most likely get a reply that makes some sort of reference to "Bitcoin". Although the terms are occasionally used in a somewhat synonymous way, they actually refer to different entities. There has been an increased awareness about Bitcoin and cryptocurrencies but do most people actually know what cryptocurrency is?

A survey conducted in August 2018 found that almost half of Americans adults are unfamiliar with Bitcoin, Ethereum, or Litecoin, and there were mixed views of where the market is headed next.[1] This exemplifies the uncertainty and newness of the market and most cryptocurrency investors today are likely just making a speculative investment.

This book starts with an introduction to key concepts of cryptocurrencies and the underlying blockchain technology. I believe that it is important for people to know exactly what cryptocurrencies are before they invest in them.

---

[1] Bitcoin, Ethereum, and Litecoin are amongst the most prominent coins on the market and are thus used as benchmarks to gauge familiarity of cryptocurrencies amongst the population.

Introduction to Blockchain and Distributed Ledger Technology

A ledger is a book of financial accounts or a record of completed transactions. Your business transactions, your bank statements, a record of your household expenses are all examples of a ledger.

Traditionally, ledgers are stored and held privately. However, blockchain technology introduces the concept of a distributed ledger. What it means for the ledger to be distributed is that you store these records across multiple sources.

For example, distributing a record of your household expenses would mean keeping an excel sheet of expenses in your computer, backing it up in a thumb drive, and printing out monthly sheets to keep in a folder. In the event that you lose one of these copies, you will still have the records somewhere.

The main benefit of distributing a ledger is reliability. You will always get access to the records as long as it is stored in this distributed "network".

Cloud computing utilises this principle of distribution so that people can access their documents, data, and websites from anywhere in the world, at any time they want.

In cloud computing, there are many servers spread around the world that are interconnected. These servers store data and records. In the event that one of these servers spoils and goes offline, access to the data is routed through the other connected and working servers. As such, cloud computing creates a reliable network of data storage.

The websites we visit every day are stored across such servers and cloud computing is the technology behind the Internet that ensures that we can have constant access to different websites and files. Picture a document or a file that is distributed across the servers. If one person loses access to the file, it is still accessible by others who have the link to the file.

Cloud computing is a service typically provided by big corporates who own servers around the world. As a cloud service provider, these companies rent out access of the servers to smaller enterprises and individual users. These customers pay the service providers for the upkeep of the file so that they can access the files any time they want.

The Problem Of Centralisation

A file that is stored on the cloud belongs to an owner. The owner can access, edit, and dictate the permissions of the file. Think of how you would use Google Drive or Dropbox to store your documents. However, the security of the files, the server uptime, and the reliability of the cloud service are all in the hands of the service provider. You may be the owner of the files but the cloud service providers still have ultimate control over them.

We trust the service providers with our data and information, although it is not exactly a choice we can make. That is the only way a typical individual can get access to cloud computing because it is very expensive and not physically feasible for him to set up a network of servers around the world.

However, the problem of centralisation is that we end up depending on these service providers but are they always reliable? If and when these organisations fail us, there will be a disruption in service, which customers already pay for and expect. A minor disruption will be a few hours of service downtime. However, a major disruption may be a permanent loss of files or loss of personal privacy.

Hackers are known to target major sites with a large number of users and a massive database. The attacks on eBay[2] and Ashley

---

[2] eBay is one of the biggest e-commerce platforms in US, so the hack impacted a significant number of users.

Madison[3] exemplifies the extent of damage where sensitive user information were compromised and hackers held the websites at ransom. Private information of many customers were leaked.

Whether it is searching on Google, connecting with others on social media, or accessing everyday websites, cloud service is the invisible force that has become so ubiquitous in our everyday lives. Consequentially, our use of these centralised services gives the service providers some power over us. For example, they can monetise our data, as did Facebook[4] and other social media sites.

In contrast, blockchain technology is a distributed network of ledgers and can function like cloud computing and a connected network of databases, with an added advantage — the quality of 'decentralisation'. That is to say, no one owns the network or the data on it.

Access to the ledgers is granted to everyone, which means that anyone can access the records and no one person will have absolute control over the ledgers. How does that work?

In the blockchain system, transactions are recorded and stored in a distributed manner and these ledgers are freely accessible. All transactions are kept transparent. In order to ensure anonymity, the accounts and transactions are represented by a complex string of numbers and digits so that it cannot be easily identifiable.

Imagine that these transactions are statements of monetary transfer. In a blockchain ledger, this would represent many anonymous accounts, with details of how much money there is in each account and transfers from one account to another. Everything is transparent and yet, you will not be able to identify the owner of each account, unless he declares his address publicly.

---

[3] Ashley Madison is a social networking app notorious for facilitating affairs amongst married individuals, so the reputation of prominent figures who used the platform was at stake.

[4] Facebook do not actually sell individual user data but rather the aggregated data of its users, which is later used for target advertisements.

As such, this application has created an anonymous and transparent monetary system, which also doubles as a decentralised storage of wealth for its users. Ledgers and tokens

> ## What is the subprime mortgage crisis?
>
> Prices of properties in the United States were steadily increasing over the decades prior to 2005-2006, and the housing market seemed infallible. More people were taking up mortgages for their homes, getting their second properties, and loans were given out more loosely. The problem was the loans issued to less than ideal homeowners, whom later defaulted on payment when the value of their houses fell below the value of their mortgage debt.
>
> The burst of the housing bubble in 2007 saw rapidly declining house prices. Although the trigger of the subprime mortgage crisis in 2008-2009 was the collapse of the housing market, it was the over-issuance of subprime (loans to people who have less than ideal credit ratings) home mortgages that exemplified the impact. The consequence was the shutdowns of financial institutions like Lehman Brothers and Bear Sterns, with hundreds of billions written off and the federal reserve stepping in to help with the crisis.
>
> When the housing bubble burst, institutions who were overly invested in providing subprime mortgage loans were the most affected as many of their subprime lenders defaulted. The insurance companies who insured the loans were also heavily affected.
>
> With the bankruptcy of Lehman Brothers and the United States government bailing out other banks, the securities and the commodities market were also heavily affected. As a whole, the concurrent collapse of all the markets had a global impact, and monetary and fiscal policies around the world had to be adjusted to cope with this financial meltdown.

on a blockchain will always be accessible and the service will always be active, as long as there are other users in the system.

Contrast this with storing money with centralised service providers like banks and safety deposit boxes. Users trust banks with the security and safety of their money and their assets, which will normally be fine. However, as the 2008 financial crisis illustrated, traditional centralised monetary institutions may not be entirely reliable. Huge sums of money were lost in the 2008 financial crisis and had to be written off. That was also when people lost faith in traditional monetary systems, which led to the creation of Bitcoin.

What is Blockchain?

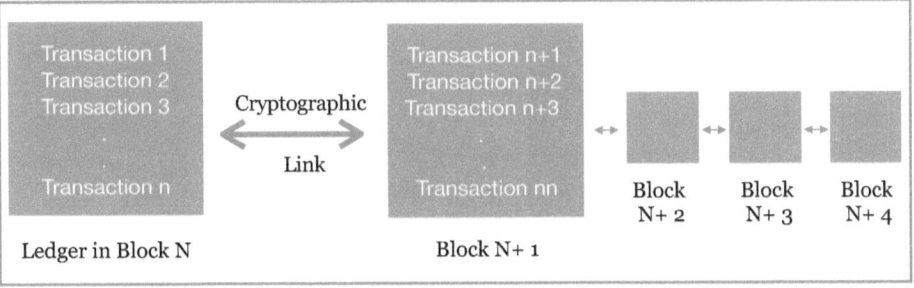

Diagram 1. The literal meaning of a blockchain.

The term "blockchain" simply describes the way that the ledger is stored. As illustrated in Diagram 1, transactions are stored in ledgers. Ledgers are stored in blocks, and blocks are connected to previous blocks, thereby forming a chain.

Cryptocurrencies are digital currencies that are built on top of blockchain technology, and the "crypto" aspect of it refers to this cryptographic link between blocks of transactions. This cryptographic link is also what makes blockchain technology secure and immutable.

For each block of transactions to be added to the previous block (which is the end of the chain), a group of users called "miners" will have to resolve the cryptography so as to connect the blocks. New blocks are constantly added and secured onto the main chain. For Bitcoin, there is one block of transactions added every 10 minutes, which we call the block time.

Miners are extremely important to the blockchain ecosystem as they are the ones who approve new transactions into the main blockchain. They are like auditors who check and validate these transactions. Miners are the people who write the ledgers.

In order to add the new block, miners have to use their computers to resolve the cryptography problem behind each transaction. When one miner successfully does that, he "inscribes" the entire block of transactions into the ledger and informs all the other miners. Thereafter, all miners have to update their ledgers with this new block and go on to resolve the next block of transactions.

The implication of having blocks after blocks of transactions that are linked cryptographically is that the whole chain of transactions cannot be altered. Once the block is confirmed, any attempt to change any details in the block would be immediately flagged out and rejected. This is the immutability quality of blockchain.

As the ledger is distributed and stored across all the miners, it would also be extremely difficult for an individual to change one instance of the ledger as the majority of the miners can prove that his version is wrong.

In actual fact, the blockchain system merely acknowledges the majority of the ledgers as the correct version. That is to say, if there are multiple versions of the ledgers, some authentic and some altered, the blockchain will recognise the greater majority as the legitimate version. That is also why we call the mining process a 'consensus mechanism' – a way for the system to agree on the right version of the ledger.

Anyone who attempts to manipulate and undermine this validation system will have to first control and influence the majority of the miners. Only when he can get a majority of the miners to vouch for his version of the ledger, will he then be able to falsify and "change" the system. Usually, this requires an extensive amount of mining resources (computing power).

The longer the history of the blocks (and the longer the chain), the more impossible it is for the malevolent miner to change the blocks because the older blocks are most likely to be recorded and stored by countless miners already. That is why blockchain is generally considered as immutable and secure.

The hostile attempt to alter the ledger as described above is called a DDOS (dedicated-denial-of-service) attack[5], which has a low probability of occurrence and typically happens to newer blocks of transactions only.

Mining is thus a form of validation – to check and inscribe new transactions. It is also a form of consensus as the miners together decide which is the correct version of the ledger. These traits are what makes the blockchain immutable and secure.

There are other methods of validation and consensus applied in different blockchain applications. In general, the key characteristics of blockchain technology can be summarised as: distributed, decentralised, immutable, and secure.

Key Qualities of a Blockchain	
Distributed	Constant uptime; everyone has a copy of it.
Decentralised	No one person or group has the rights over it.
Immutable	It cannot be edited or changed.
Secure	It is not easy for malicious players to disrupt it.

Blockchain technology is just an instance of distributed ledgers. There are other distributed ledger systems where the ledgers are distributed across multiple users, and which are not stored in blocks or in a chain. Hence, blockchain technology is merely a subset of the wider term "distributed ledger technology" (DLT).

Compared to traditional databases, DLT is an alternative way of storing data, values, and transactions. The distributed ledgers can contain monetary transactions, data transactions, ownership

---

[5] If a mining pool accumulates more than 51% of the mining power, it does not necessitate a DDOS attack. It merely hints at the probability of such an attack.

records, and any other types of transactional records. Hence, the significance of DLT lies in its potential to transform transactional processes.

In 2009, Satoshi Nakamoto introduced a system of peer-to-peer cash transfer. He created tokens on top of the blockchain technology and called it Bitcoin. These tokens represented a system of money. The Bitcoin blockchain recorded trading and transfers of Bitcoin tokens from one account to another and the ledgers are validated by Bitcoin miners.

To incentivise miners to continually validate new transactions, new Bitcoin tokens were created and issued to miners. Only the first miner who successfully adds the new block is rewarded with a block reward in Bitcoins.

Hence, it became a competitive game where miners competed with one another to add new blocks of transactions to the Bitcoin blockchain so as to earn Bitcoins. The miners then sold their Bitcoins on the market to reimburse their mining expenses.

Bitcoin was the first instance of a cryptocurrency.

Besides utilising the cryptography technique and a distributed ledger, Bitcoin added a layer of tokens on top of the blockchain technology. This also created a new use case of DLT – as a form of decentralised money.

What Satoshi Nakamoto created was not just a system of digital money. He created an ecosystem of developers, miners, and users. In this system, the developers maintained the code while the miners validated the transactions and indirectly introduce new coins into the system when they are rewarded. The price value of the Bitcoin tokens are collectively determined by coin owners and users, which forms the demand and supply of the coins.

A system of money merely accounts for who owes who what and who owns how much. In comparison, an ecosystem of money is not only about the ledgers but also involves the different stakeholders and how their actions are intertwined.

Cryptocurrencies – A Use Case of DLT

Keeping the notion of Bitcoin and blockchain tokens in mind, it is important to note that blockchain and DLT can exist without tokens. For example, there are private blockchains (or permissioned blockchain[6]) where either no tokens are involved or they are held privately. These private blockchains capitalise on the immutability and security of the blockchain technology to improve on their existing database storage functions.

Satoshi created Bitcoin (BTC) in 2009 with the idea of a "Peer-to-Peer Electronic Cash System"[7]. It was the period of the aftermath of the Lehman Brother's collapse. The subprime mortgage crisis revealed many flaws in the existing financial systems and people were uncertain about trusting their money with banks. It was this loss of trust in centralised financial institutions that led to the uprise of a decentralised system.

How could investment banks lose hundreds of billions in dollars, require the government to step in, write off billions in dollars, and affect the global market so severely? Why do we still trust these centralised organisations?

Bitcoin was the first cryptocurrency that surfaced and it has since inspired many other copycats. Given its open-sourced nature, it is relatively easy for someone to duplicate the blockchain system. The question is whether others would assign a value to the copycat version and why they would choose the counterpart over the original Bitcoin.

Many other cryptocurrencies have since arisen, each promising an advantage over the original Bitcoin. Litecoin (LTC) for example utilises a different cryptographic script, has four times the supply, and shorter block validation times. The purpose was to create a

---

[6] Bitcoin is thus an example of a public or permissionless blockchain.

[7] The idea of a peer-to-peer digital cash has been going around for several years already. It was the subprime mortgage crisis that prompted the uptake of the Bitcoin.

currency that can accommodate faster transaction rates so that LTC tokens can be used for everyday payments.

Ethereum (ETH) on the other hand popularised the term 'smart contract'. Ethereum emphasised on the opportunity for DLT to be the middleman of transactions. Smart contract is simply an agreement governed and secured by the blockchain technology so that two parties can trust each other to fulfil their parts of the transaction without the need to go through a middleman.

Today, blockchain and DLT is not just about monetary transfers from an account to another. DLT can support any kind of data transfer, which means that any digital files, ownership, records, or values can be stored and shared openly.

The Cryptocurrency Market

Besides being a digital token, cryptocurrency is unique as these tokens can be traded on a market. Buyers and sellers agree on a price and exchange ownership of these tokens. The cryptocurrency market is thus formed from the exchange of all the different tokens, which is pretty much like a stock market where stocks are traded from one person to another.

Stocks are a form of security. If you own the stock, it gives you the right of ownership to a small portion of the company. Similarly, if you own the cryptocurrencies, you have the right of ownership over that quantity of cryptocurrencies.

On another hand, cryptocurrencies can be used as money just like fiat currencies. Although it is not as widely accepted as the Dollars, Pounds, and Euros, it is still a form of currency in places that accept this mode of payment. In this monetary perspective, the cryptocurrency market is like a money changer where you exchange from one cryptocurrency to another.

To date, there is not a single definition to cryptocurrencies because their day-to-day applications span across different functions. Most online sources generally agree that cryptocurrencies are either a Currency, Security Token, or Utility Token but as the United States

Securities Exchange Commission (SEC) have clarified, it all depends on what investors are expecting when they purchased the tokens, and the classification of the tokens can change over time[8].

i. Currency

As a currency, the price of cryptocurrencies is derived from the demand and supply of the coins on the free market. Despite being mildly accepted today, people buy cryptocurrencies because they believe that it has a monetary value that is undervalued today. They believe that cryptocurrencies will eventually be adopted and they will then be able to use it to exchange for products and services, just like fiat currencies.

ii. Securities

As a form of security, cryptocurrency represents the rights to the ownership of a company or some of its assets. People buy security-type cryptocurrencies like they would stocks of a company as they believe that these tokens will become more valuable when the company grows, which is very much like buying stocks of a company.

iii. Utility Tokens

Cryptocurrencies that fall under this category do not represent money or the rights of ownership. Instead, they are credits issued by a company, which users purchase in order to exchange for products and services offered by the company.

Think of iTunes or Amazon Store credits, or chips in a casino, where you acquire these credits so as to participate in that particular company's offered activities. They cannot be used outside of these systems. The main difference between these credits and cryptocurrency tokens is that the latter is built on top of the blockchain technology.

---

[8] As new applications are constantly being developed, a token originally designed to be a currency may end up being a security or utility token.

Today, cryptocurrencies that are classified as utility tokens have way more complicated uses than a mere credit system to exchange for the company's services. Regardless of their categories, the fact that over 1,500 different cryptocurrencies[9] are being traded on the market creates an opportunity for investors to profit by trading cryptocurrencies.

As the use cases of cryptocurrencies continue to expand, it is evident that this classification has to improve in order to keep up with the rapidly changing crypto space. This was also why I came up with an alternative way of categorising cryptocurrencies (in Chapter 4) that better accounts for their respective functions and the risks associated with each function.

---

[9] The are in fact many more cryptocurrencies. However, online aggregators typically capture only those listed on coin exchanges, so many ICO tokens and private tokens are omitted from this number.

Cryptocurrencies – A New Technology Paradigm

In the nineteenth century, the Industrial Revolution led to the uprise of machines. Widespread adoption of automation greatly reduced the need and demand for manual labour. Then, computers and cell phones came into the picture, which changed the way people worked and communicated. It transformed the economy and created boundless opportunities.

Computers rapidly became more portable and powerful, and when the Internet and the World Wide Web arrived towards the end of the twentieth century, the Internet Revolution changed the way that information was shared. What used to be stored within a computer and transferred around in physical copies of diskettes and compact discs (CDs) are now uploaded online and easily accessible from anywhere. The Internet has transformed the way knowledge is stored and disseminated, and it has also enabled real-time communication amongst people.

Our world today would be a high-tech, science-fiction dream to the people of the nineteenth century. Nonetheless, what we should take away is that each of these technologies transformed the way that people lived. These technologies have been so impactful that people are forced to adapt to it.

Even the advent of smartphone applications, which is a relatively minor technological upgrade, has changed the way we consume services. From ride-hailing to food delivery and even traveling and holidays, service industries worldwide have been disrupted by apps. Everything is now accessible at the touch of your fingertips.

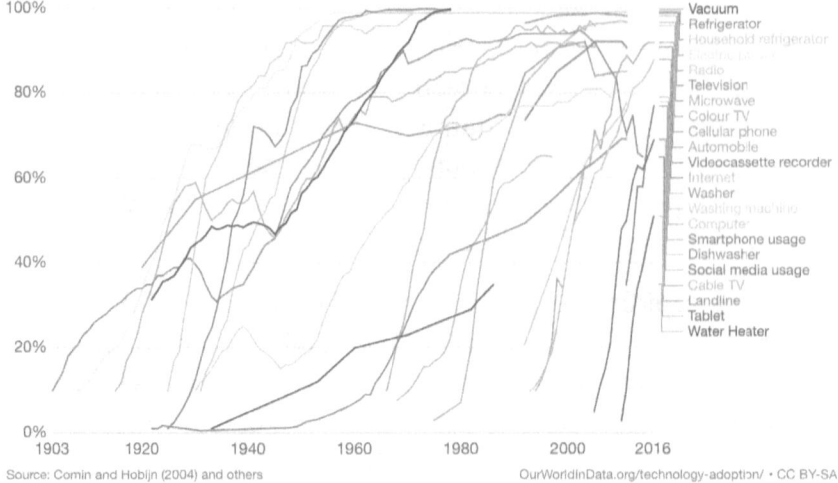

Diagram 2. The rapidly increasing rate of technology adoption[10].

One commonly talked about chart is the rate of technology adoption, which has become shorter across the years (the chart lines are more vertical than diagonal). That is to say, new technologies are being adopted by the masses more quickly today.

If we were to put cryptocurrencies onto this chart, the technology has already been operating and evolving in the past decade. Many people thus believe that cryptocurrencies and blockchain technology will be widely adopted in the next five years.

Despite that belief, we have to keep in mind that cryptocurrencies are still evolving and new applications are still popping up. Today, the two main uses of cryptocurrencies are as a form of money and for smart contracts. The significance of decentralisation is that it transforms a fundamental aspect of our daily lives – transactions – and this revolution can be as impactful as that of the machines, the computers, and the Internet.

---

[10] The tablet and smartphone took just several years to be widely adopted, so cryptocurrencies are often thought to follow this pattern.

i. Digital Currency – A standardised and decentralised form of money

The long-standing and most easily understood application of cryptocurrency is that it is a universal form of money that is not owned by any centralised entity. Unlike fiat currencies that are regulated by governments, Bitcoin was designed to be decentralised – to be free from the control of banks and centralised institutions.

To be adopted as a universal currency, Bitcoin has to be widely accepted. The idealised scenario is that users will no longer have to transfer from one fiat currency to another as they travel across the globe because they can use cryptocurrencies wherever they go. Foreign workers will also have a standardised form of money that they can remit back home without having to go through multiple intermediaries that charge expensive transaction fees. This has the potential to cut out PayPal, SWIFT transfers, Western Union[11] and other financial intermediaries.

Theoretically, cryptocurrency transactions should incur lower transaction fees and are processed more quickly than traditional monetary transactions. However, there are current limitations in the blockchain system and this is not entirely true, for now[12].

The bigger implication of cryptocurrencies is decentralisation, which presents a vastly different ideological practice where your money is not governed, controlled, or monitored by someone. When the economy is doing well and centralised institutions are reliable, it is hard to imagine cryptocurrency as an alternative form of money. Why would we change a system that is not broken?

What cryptocurrencies propose instead is that users can exchange and trade directly with one another, much like the older days of

---

[11] PayPal, SWIFT, and Western Union help facilitate money exchange and transfer, and charge a percentage fee of the transaction.

[12] In the December 2017 bull market, pending transactions were aplenty and coin prices were sky high, which led to network congestion in transactions and expensive transaction fees as they were paid in coins.

barter trade. There is an agreed upon value on everyday things and people can independently conduct peer-to-peer transactions without the need to go through a monetary system. The value of these transactions will not be measured in dollars or any other government-controlled money but in cryptocurrencies.

The plausibility of this alternative monetary system signifies a new paradigm of how society and the use of money can operate independently. There is also now an alternative way to store monetary value, whereas traditional methods would involve the buying of assets like gold, art, or properties.

The only gripe about this alternative form of money is that it is currently unregulated. This means that we might still be subjected to regulatory rules in the use of cryptocurrencies in future and we are not protected if we were to lose our cryptocurrencies.

ii. Smart Contracts – Reliable, trustable, and blockchain-mediated transactions

Besides facilitating an account of money, blockchain and DLT can be used to mediate any value transfer between two bodies. This means that DLT mediates the exchange of ownership rights, documents, or any form of data, between two people, between individuals and an organisation, or between two organisations.

Imagine a reliable and trustable system that is not governed by anyone. This could be selling your house or car to someone and receiving payment without going through an agent. It could be a transfer of money, data, or sensitive information between an individual and an organisation reliably, securely, and anonymously.

In today's world, these transactions are usually facilitated by third-party intermediaries who charge a fee for their services. Alibaba and PayPal, for example, has an escrow service to mediate the transactions between a supplier and a customer. To buy your groceries, book a hotel, or pay for any other services online, you likely have to go through Mastercard or Visa who charge a transaction fee on the merchants' end. Blockchain threatens to cut out all these middlemen so the sellers will transact directly with the customers.

There are many other use cases of smart contracts and it really can be applied to anything transactional in our everyday lives. While these processes can be transformed, it is important to note that you do not have to invest in cryptocurrencies to benefit from the eventual use of it.

Even if Bitcoin does become stable and widely accepted, using $10 worth of BTC then will only get you an equivalent value in service or product. It will not cost you more to use cryptocurrencies if it becomes the golden standard of transactions. That is to say, your belief and support for cryptocurrencies do not have to translate to an investment.

Instead, investors today are participating in the market to grow their money. They may be championing the adoption of cryptocurrencies but the reason they buy cryptocurrencies today is really to use this technology opportunity to grow their wealth.

Cryptocurrency As An Investment

A financial investment is an entity that you put money into in order to gain profits. You can invest in assets and commodities. You can invest in financial products, stocks or derivatives. The common goal is to grow money and different types of investments help you to grow money in different ways.

For example, investments in assets act as a store of value against the dollar. Investments in stocks may generate a dividend yield on top of capital appreciation. Investments in savings plans and government bonds are low-risk and low-yielding but help to counter annual inflation, while investments in derivatives can help you hedge against your other investments.

Today, new cryptocurrencies are still coming to the market. Bitcoin future contracts have been launched while other crypto-related derivatives are still being developed and seeking approval. It is plausible that you will be able to get a similar form of hedging, dividend-yield, and capital-appreciation types of crypto investment products on the market eventually.

Each investment vehicle carries a certain set of risks. As a general rule of thumb, if you are looking for bigger ROIs (return on investments), you have to bear greater risks.

Compared to other high-risk investments, cryptocurrencies offer the potential of a proportionately larger return. This relates to a higher risk-reward ratio, which means that you stand to reap a proportionately bigger reward for the same dollar that you risk losing.

However, it would also mean that you bear more risk on crypto investments, which includes greater volatility, high incidence of hacks and scams, and regulatory risks. An investment with a high risk-reward ratio but a low winning frequency can still lead to losses over the long run[13].

---

[13] For example, if you risk $1 to earn $3 for each trade but is only successful 20% of the time, you will make $60 (20*3) and lose $80 (80*1), your net gain after 100 trades is negative $20.

That is why you have to be familiar with cryptocurrencies to minimise these risks. You have to pick the right cryptocurrencies that have a better chance of appreciating and the likelihood of surviving in the long run.

There are many ways that you can profit from cryptocurrencies and this book aims to break down the different strategies to better suit your investing style. Personally, I use a qualitative approach to assess the mid to long-term potential of cryptocurrencies, complemented with trading strategies to time my entries and exits.

Besides giving you a brief overview of the cryptocurrencies and the underlying technology, the goal of this book is to get you acquainted and comfortable with the buying and selling of a volatile asset. Subsequently, you can go on to learn about using other types of analyses to up your game.

There are several assumptions held when writing this book.

1. Longevity of cryptocurrencies
   DLT is a technology and cryptocurrencies is an application that is here to stay, hence there will always be a value to cryptocurrencies.

2. Eventual adoption of cryptocurrencies
   Cryptocurrencies is mildly accepted and recognised today. When they are widely adopted and accepted, the market value of cryptocurrencies will generally increase.

3. The value of scarcity
   The fact that there is a limited quantity of coins means that holding some of it deprives others of the same supply. Hence, if it is valuable and it will appreciate over time.

4. Regulations help, not kill
   Cryptocurrency is beneficial. Institutions should be working on frameworks to foster adoption safely and effectively instead of disabling or banning cryptocurrencies.

Chapter Summary

Cryptocurrency is a particular use case of DLT that has arisen in the aftermath of the subprime mortgage crisis. It has come about because people have lost trust in centralised institutions and cryptocurrencies can mediate trust between two or more bodies. Today, cryptocurrencies are most commonly used as a form of money or as a smart contract.

As a technology, cryptocurrency has the potential to transform our way of life by changing the way we transact with one another. However, that alone does not make it investment worthy. It is the opportunity of buying in ahead of the pack and the potential of generating huge returns that makes cryptocurrencies an attractive investment.

However, your investment in cryptocurrencies will be highly risky and you will have to bear extreme price volatility and uncertainties in the development of the technology and in regulations. As such, it is important to understand how blockchain technology works and the ecosystem behind cryptocurrencies.

From my experience, people often buy cryptocurrency without understanding it thoroughly. When the market takes a downturn, these people are the ones who have second thoughts about their crypto investments and often end up selling off their cryptocurrencies at a loss or only aim to break even. Then, they remove themselves from the crypto space entirely.

This book was written to help you understand the technology, the market forces, and key issues in the crypto space. By sharing simple qualitative and quantitative investment techniques, I hope to advocate for a healthy way of investing so that you can grow your wealth, and most importantly, live to experience all of these.

Chapter 2
Getting Started On Cryptocurrencies

Where can we buy and sell some coins?
How do we go about it?

There are a few methods to get your first cryptocurrency. It involves buying cryptocurrency with your fiat currency. This is typically done via a fiat-to-crypto coin exchange, a peer-to-peer (P2P) trade, or over-the-counter (OTC) methods.

Most investors start off buying either Bitcoin (BTC) or Ethereum (ETH) with fiat currency. This is because there are many altcoins that cannot be traded directly with fiat and can only be traded with the main cryptocurrencies like BTC and ETH.

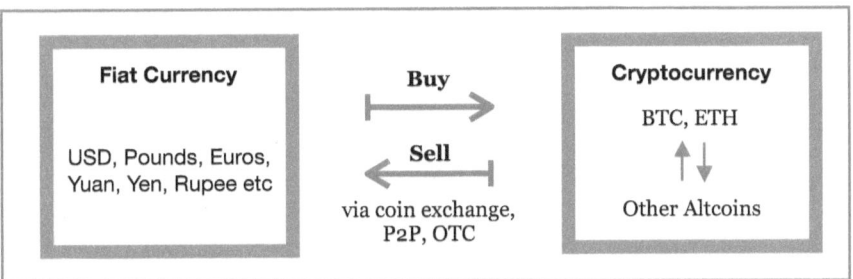

Diagram 3. Buying and selling of cryptocurrencies.

In order to be profitable on your investment, you must sell your cryptocurrency for a higher price than you bought it at. Similarly, the price of the altcoins must appreciate against BTC or ETH for your altcoin investments to be profitable.

Hence, when we look at cryptocurrency as an investment today, a key factor is the selling of your cryptocurrency, unless you are planning to keep the cryptocurrencies for many years until they are adopted as a mainstream standard for payment.

This is where the liquidity of cryptocurrencies matters. Liquidity refers to how easy it is to convert your investment into a liquid asset, in this case, money.

The more prominent cryptocurrencies like Bitcoin and Ethereum are generally more liquid as they are more widely bought and sold. In comparison, altcoins are less liquid and you may have to convert them into BTC or ETH first before selling those for fiat money.

When signing up with coin exchanges, you should consider the type of cryptocurrencies they offer and also the daily trading volume on the exchanges. Registering on bigger coin exchanges with larger buy and sell volumes will mean that you can liquidate your cryptocurrencies more readily.

Buying Your First Cryptocurrency

i. Fiat-to-crypto coin exchanges

International branches of fiat-to-cryptocurrency exchanges typically support a few cryptocurrencies paired with many fiat currencies. That is to say, you can typically get only Bitcoin or Ethereum on these exchanges but you can buy and sell it with many supported fiat currencies.

For example, CoinBase currently supports four different cryptocurrencies that can be bought with over 30 different international fiat currencies.

On the other hand, smaller localised coin exchanges tend to support more cryptocurrencies paired with only one or two fiat currency. You can get about 10 different cryptocurrencies on these exchanges but they may only support the local fiat currency.

Usually, these smaller coin exchanges only support users from their region so you will likely have to show proof of residency when you register on these exchanges. This strict KYC (know-your-customer) procedure is enforced by the local government in order to circumvent money laundering.

Notable ones are CoinBase, GDAX, Gemini, Bitfinex, Kraken, Bitstamp, CoinHako (Singapore/Malaysia), Bitthumb (Korea), Coinone (Korea), bitFlyer (Japan), Coincheck (Japan), Luno (Asia), CoinSpot (Australia), TokoCrypto (Indonesia).

Do check out the smaller exchanges that support your region. The time taken to verify your identity on exchanges can range from days to weeks and prices can fluctuate a lot in that period.

As verification on coin exchanges can take a while, it is thus something that you can start on while reading up on blockchain technology and cryptocurrencies.

ii. Over-the-counter and peer-to-peer

If you are looking to avoid the exorbitant transaction fees of coin exchanges, you can use OTC and P2P methods to buy and sell directly from other users.

It is generally cheaper and relatively safe if you are familiar with using a cryptocurrency wallet and the transaction process. You meet up in person, the seller sends you the cryptocurrency, and you pay them in cash or bank transfer upon receiving the coins.

These sellers usually charge a percentage fee that is lower than any coin exchanges. This is much like a cash-on-delivery method and a similar reversed process applies if you are looking to sell cryptocurrencies.

Miners prefer to sell their mined cryptocurrencies via OTC and P2P methods as they have to sell regularly and would want to avoid the transaction fees of coin exchanges.

However, this type of transaction is highly unregulated and not monitored. There is a chance that the money or cryptocurrency that you are getting may have been ill-gotten. You could unknowingly be playing a role in money laundering when someone pays you dirty money in return for your cryptocurrencies.

As this is a grey area, I would not delve further into where you can buy or sell via these methods. In future, there may also be regulations that clamp down on such transactions and deem them as illegal.

Buying and Selling Altcoins

There are over thousands of cryptocurrencies and those that are not mainstream are considered altcoins, or alternative coins. The rise of ICOs in 2017 have greatly increased the number of altcoins in the cryptocurrency market.

> ## What is an ICO?
>
> Initial Coin Offerings (ICO) came about as a use case for smart contracts. In an ICO, investors pledge an amount of Bitcoin or Ethereum in return for a number of the new coins. One major use case for this is to use cryptocurrencies as a fundraising tool.
>
> For example, X company launches an ICO using a smart contract that stipulates that you will get 100 Coin X for 1 ETH pledged. After collecting 10,000 ETH, X company will issue 1,000,000 Coin X. They will go on to build their product with this capital, and when Coin X is ready for use, investors can then exchange Coin X for services offered by the company, or resell it.
>
> Unlike IPOs that require a strict legal and audit process that cost millions in dollars, you simply need to write a White Paper to conduct an ICO. The White Paper is like a business plan that explains your company, product, and strategy. Then, you set up the digital smart contract, and if you successfully raise the desired amount, the contract is automatically executed. You get the pledged BTC and ETH and you issue the new coins to the pledgers.
>
> ICOs democratise the creation of tokens. As a result, many new altcoins have emerged — be it legitimate, fake, scam, or weak coins.

i. Crypto-to-crypto coin exchanges

To trade for altcoins, you will likely have to register on crypto-to-crypto coin exchanges. The KYC procedure on these exchanges tends to be looser since you are trading a digital asset for another. Typically, you will also not be able to trade cryptocurrencies to and fro fiat currencies on these exchanges, which is an anti-laundering measure.

The upside is that you will get access to a huge variety of coins and ICO tokens that can be bought with your ETH or BTC coins.

Each exchange has its own set of security measures and protocols. They also have a different variance in their spread, which means that the difference between the buy and sell price of a particular cryptocurrency can be very big. Coin exchanges profit from this spread and some exchanges are known to have over 10% of variance in their spread.

As a general rule of thumb, you will want to pick exchanges with bigger trading volume as they tend to be more reliable. Bigger volumes also allow these exchanges to have a smaller spread and still make profits. Lastly, the bigger exchanges tend to invest more in their security protocols.

To find out which exchanges offer your desired cryptocurrency, simply check out CoinMarketCap.com. Notable crypto-to-crypto coin exchanges are Binance, Upbit, Huobi, OKEx, Poloneix, Bitfinex, Bithumb, Bittrex, GDAX, Kraken, HitBTC etc.

ii. Atomic swaps and decentralised exchanges

The problem with trading cryptocurrencies via coin exchanges is that these exchanges are centralised companies. They have custody of your coins if you store the coins on their wallets and they have information about trading patterns and trading volume. Coin exchanges are also known to use trading bots to maintain the trading volume of lesser-known cryptocurrencies.

This brings us back to the initial problems of centralisation. Are we over-empowering these coin exchanges?

Today, we are looking at newer methods of cryptocurrency trading where users trade directly with one another without going through a coin exchange. For example, Bitcoin to Ethereum atomic swaps have already been successfully implemented. There are also companies that are working on creating decentralised exchanges (DEX) so that users can swap their altcoins directly with another user based on the existing market rate.

The irony about buying and storing of cryptocurrencies on coin exchanges is that we are aiming to achieve decentralisation but we still trust centralised exchanges so much. Perhaps, it is inevitable that we have to go through this phase of centralisation before we can eventually hit a decentralised stage. For now, we have to wait till the arrival and uptake of DEXs in order to achieve true decentralisation.

> ### How are coins stored? Where do they exist?
>
> While the bank stores money and gold in their safes, cryptocurrencies are stored in the virtual system and segmented into different partitions. A wallet is a partition in this system. Having your own private wallet means you have the keys to your partition. Think of the system as a big safe, and within it, you have a dedicated safe called your wallet.
>
> Coin exchanges have their dedicated safes where they store all the coins of their users. Within their safe, they create partitions for you to use. Should they be hacked, the exchange's entire library of safes will be compromised.
>
> Within each safe partition, there is a public wallet address and a private key. The public address is an identifier, like a tag number for that safe, which you can tell others about so they know where to send coins to you. Then there is a private key, which you should keep absolutely secret.
>
> The private key is used to sign withdrawals from your safe. Hence when you are sending coins to someone, your transaction hash (receipt) specifies a quantity of coins from one public address to another, along with other transaction details. It is only authorised when you sign the transaction with your private key.
>
> Do not ever disclose your private keys to anyone. Your private keys should be treated as importantly as your security PINs and online passwords.

Storage of Cryptocurrencies

Most newcomers will likely store their cryptocurrencies on the default wallets provided by the coin exchanges. It is highly recommended to take your coins off the exchanges' wallets and into your own private wallet.

If you store your coins on an exchange, you are entrusting the custody of your coins to a centralised coin exchange. Should the exchange go down, your coins will be gone too. Exchanges are generally reliable but they hold a lot of user funds, which makes them prime targets for hackers. Hence, if you store your coins on the exchange, you run the risk of the exchange going bankrupt, being hacked, or the company absconding with all your coins.

If you are planning to execute short-term trades, where the duration is in weeks and months, it still makes sense to store your coins on the exchange. This is because the withdrawal of coins from an exchange typically incurs a high transaction fee. However, if you plan to hold the cryptocurrencies for more than a year, you should take them off the exchange and store them in your private wallet.

There are several types of private wallets available — software-based, hardware-based, and paper wallets. The minimum recommended is to use a software-based wallet so that the security keys (your private address) are stored on your device.

Given that your device with the private keys can still be compromised, you can choose to store them in an offline method to be extra secure. For example, it can be written on a paper, stored in a hardware-based wallet, or on a QR code printed on paper. Distributing your keys and passwords in multiple places is a form of security backup.

1. Software wallets
   Software-based cryptocurrency wallets require you to install plug-ins or programmes onto your device (usually a laptop). Your addresses and keys are stored and encrypted by the

software, so you will only need to remember your account and password instead of having to write down the long string of characters. You do have to trust the service providers of the software wallets, and you have to take enough precautionary measures to protect and backup your personal device.

2. Hardware wallets

    The most commonly used hardware wallets are the Trezor and the Ledger. These are USB devices that store and encrypt your address and keys, and accessible via a PIN. During set up, you will be required to make a back up on paper and when using the wallet, your connected computer will not store any of the data. Hence, it is generally considered the gold standard for storing and accessing of cryptocurrencies.

3. Paper wallets

    You can actually set up your own address and private keys manually, although it will require more technical expertise. Paper wallets like MyEtherWallet will help you to set it up and you can eventually write down or print out the private keys and the backup seed words. If you do decide to embark on this, remember to make multiple backups, and do not store the passwords, seeds, or private keys on a Notes app or a digital document on your device just for convenience sake.

If you have already decided to learn about and invest in cryptocurrencies, it will require marginally more effort to set up and store your cryptocurrencies securely. Alternatively, you can choose to have convenience and security by forking out around $100 for a hardware wallet. It is a small price to pay for the ease of mind that you will be getting.

Chapter Summary

There are different channels to acquire your first cryptocurrencies and most people start off by buying Bitcoin or Ethereum. Subsequently, you should transfer the cryptocurrencies out of the exchanges and store them in your private wallet if you are looking to hold it for more than a year. There are several types of private wallets available and the hardware wallet is the gold standard for storing and accessing of cryptocurrencies.

The cryptocurrencies you plan to buy and the coin exchanges you register with affects the liquidity of your investment. Hence, it is important to look into the different coin exchanges that service your region before you start investing in cryptocurrencies.

Towards the end of the book, I will bring up past instances of hacks on cryptocurrency exchanges to remind you of the importance of storing your coins safely. You will eventually be very familiar with the buying and selling of cryptocurrencies so do take some time to get yourself ready for the long investment journey ahead.

II: Mad As A Hatter – Crypto Investing Essentials

"I could tell you my adventures — beginning from this morning," said Alice a little timidly, "but it's no use going back to yesterday, because I was a different person then."

Chapter 3
Investing Is About Active Risk Management
How can we safely and effectively invest in the crypto market?

Determining Your Risk Profile

Before embarking on any types of investments, it is important to ask yourself these two questions:

1. How much excess capital can you afford to take out or set aside for investments, so as to maintain your current lifestyle?

2. How much can you afford to invest, assuming you were to lose it all?

Start by listing down the commitments in your life and set aside your required expenditure. These should be your priority.

Do you have loans or debts to service? Do you have a relationship or a family to support? What are your monthly expenses? Do you have seasonal expenses? How much money do you earn and how much do you need to get by? Do you have emergency funds for healthcare or accidents, and are you covered by insurance?

Once you have accounted for the necessities, you will have the remainder, which you have to split across your savings, your luxury expenses, and entire investment portfolio. **The next question is, what proportion of the remainder should you invest into cryptocurrencies?**

To answer that question, we should look at your risk appetite.

People with larger risk appetites would be comfortable with dedicating a proportionately larger sum of money to high-risk investments. On another hand, risk-averse individuals would likely prefer the low-risk-low-returns kind of investments.

We should also look at alternative forms of investments in terms of their associated risk and rewards and determine if cryptocurrency investing is really for you. Trading of options and futures is a viable alternative to cryptocurrency for investors with large risk appetites. For low-risk investors, cryptocurrency should be avoided entirely or take up only a very small portion of your entire investment portfolio.

With these considerations in mind, you can go on to allocate a portion of your income or savings into cryptocurrencies. The plus side is that there is no minimum amount required for cryptocurrency investments.

Laying Down Your Ground Rules

Before you start, it is important to establish your own investing principles. This will be a handy set of guidelines that you can turn to whenever you need to make a major investment decision.

Your investment principles should be personal and tailored to your risk profile and risk appetite. As we go through my personal ground rules below, feel free to adapt it or remove any of the points that you disagree with.

1. Invest only what you can lose.
   All investments are risky; cryptocurrency is even riskier. Invest an amount that you are prepared to lose entirely without putting you in debt or affecting your life detrimentally. Do not take loans or mortgages to invest in cryptocurrencies.

2. Investing is different from trading.
   Trading involves actively monitoring the market and making profits from smaller price differences. Investing takes on a more long-term position, which means picking good fundamentals and looking at long-term trends.

3. Do not make hasty, emotional-based decision.
   The market can move rapidly especially for cryptocurrencies. The wild price fluctuations can affect emotions and impede decision-making ability. Recognise when that happens, take a break before and stabilise your emotions before executing any trades. It is okay to lose out on the trade meanwhile.

4. Identify and keep in mind your investment goal.
   Are you trying to grow your retirement funds? Are you creating a passive stream of income or are you trading for a living? Your eventual investment strategy will be dependent on your goals.

5. Cash is a position.
   You may have exited while the market continued to rise, or you may have missed a dip. Remember, cash is a position and you will always have more opportunities ahead.

6. Recognise that hindsight is 20/20.
   The market might have moved against your expectations but you do not have to beat yourself up over it. On hindsight, everything will seem obvious and "you should have known". Instead, reflect on how differently you would act if a similar situation were to arise and avoid making the same mistakes.

7. Recognise the concept of opportunity cost.
   We have limited resources and the opportunity cost of investing in a particular entity is that you cannot put that sunk amount into other investments. It is perfectly okay to miss out on certain trades because you made your decision based on the availability of existing information then.

Generic Strategies for Cryptocurrency Investing

There are a few ways that you can grow your investment capital. Each method demands a different amount of time and resources in researching and monitoring the cryptocurrency market so you should choose the ones that are most suitable for you.

Buy And Hold	Reap Dividends	Moon With Alts	Core And Peripheries
Long-Term	Mid To Long-Term	Short-Term	Long-Term
Least effortful. Can simply average the buy and sell orders.	**Some effort.** Requires more researching at the beginning.	**Very effortful.** Need to constantly monitor price actions.	**Very effortful.** Need to look for coins, monitor price actions, and constantly make trades to grow "Core"
BTC, ETH, Crypto ETFs	BTC, Selected Altcoins	Altcoins	BTC/ETH + Selected Altcoins

Table 1. Overview of crypto investing strategies.

i. Long-term buy and HODL

The simplest strategy is to buy Bitcoin alongside Ethereum and keep them for the long term. If you believe that blockchain technology and cryptocurrencies will eventually be adopted, their prices will rise just like the technology-based stocks did in the millennium after the Dot Com Bubble. This is the most direct and no-brainer way to invest.

You will not need much time and effort to keep track of the prices. You can go in at any price and go in periodically. The overall long-term price value of cryptocurrencies will be higher in the future so any price now is a good price.

Alternatively, you can also choose to put your money in cryptocurrency-based ETFs (exchange-traded funds) and indexes, which are currently unavailable but likely to be implemented in future. These funds spread out your investment across the top 20 or 30 coins so your investment will be tantamount to investing in cryptocurrencies in general.

ii. Reaping the dividends

There are several cryptocurrencies that pay out a number of derivative coins. Coin holders are rewarded with these derivatives much like dividend payouts for shareholders of stocks. However, these derivative coins may or may not have substantial value.

> ### What is a hard fork?
>
> In cryptocurrency, a fork occurs when there is a new implementation to the code to change certain rules or protocol. For example, it can be changes to the mining rules, coin supply, block size, or new features. It is similar to a software update for your operating systems or mobile app versions.
>
> A soft fork is a backward-compatible, reversible implementation. It is like a beta mode that can be rolled back and non-permanent. A hard fork, however, is a permanent integration to the existing code. A hard fork is usually sealed in after a period of soft fork and is activated when the new code base is shown to be stable and accepted by a significant majority.
>
> During the implementation of a hard fork, if the network disagrees on the changes, it may lead to a split. There will henceforth be two different coins. One group of developers and miners will support the newly forked coin while another group chooses to abide by the old rules and stick with the original system and coin.
>
> Forks can be taken positively as it signals that there is development in the coin and hence there are different beliefs in the path to adoption. However, the ecosystem of developers and miners will be divided between servicing the newly forked coin and the original coin so there will always be a period of uncertainty and instability right after the coin splits.

Another way to reap the dividends is to invest in major coins and wait for their forks. Forks occur when a particular cryptocurrency deviates from its main chain into an alternative chain, leading to two different cryptocurrencies. At the point of the fork, if you hold ONE coin, you will have ONE coin on the main chain and ONE coin on the alternative chain after the fork.

Do note that not all forks lead to a split. There were hard forks that have been executed like system upgrades, and there were no coin splits because majority of the community agreed with the upgrade.

Notable Bitcoin forks are Bitcoin Cash (BCH) and Bitcoin Gold (BTG) while the major forked Ethereum coin is Ethereum Classic (ETC). Simply by holding on to Bitcoin or Ethereum at the point of the forks, you will get an equivalent number of the forked coin. Subsequently, you can sell off the forked coins for profits and keep your main coins for future forks.

iii. Shooting to the moon with alts

Venture capitalist (VC) firms invest in many startups but not every one of them will succeed. Given that over 90% of startup companies fail, VCs have to carefully evaluate and only invest in startups that have the potential to generate over 10 times in ROI. This way, even if only 1 in 10 of their invested companies succeeds, they will still make good on their investments.

Altcoins are similar to startup companies in their potential to "moon" – a slang used to describe an exponential growth. While startup companies idealise a hockey-stick growth in users or in revenue, the prices of altcoins also have the potential to grow exponentially.

Hence, mooning with alts takes on a similar strategy as the VCs by placing your bets strategically in multiple altcoins and waiting for them to pay off. It is still a highly speculative investment so you have to minimise your risk by properly assessing the business behind these altcoins. Otherwise, it is no different from gambling as you have over 1,500 different cryptocurrencies to "invest" in.

iv. Core and peripheries

Most people start with Bitcoin or Ethereum and expand upon their initial investment by picking a variety of altcoins. This strategy involves holding one main cryptocurrency and several 'peripheries' to complement the main cryptocurrency.

This strategy reduces risk through diversification in altcoins. Furthermore, there is a good chance to get a better than average performance by holding the altcoins, which will be your peripheral tool for growing your investment.

One variation of this strategy is to use the peripheral altcoins to build up your long-term holding of core coins like Bitcoin or Ethereum. You capitalise on the wild fluctuations of altcoins and sell when they appreciate against Bitcoin or Ethereum. When these peripheries have realised their growth potential, you switch to a new selection of peripheries with more potential and over time, you aim to increase your principal amount of core coins.

This method is resource intensive as it requires you to constantly monitor the price of peripheries against the price of the cores. Moreover, you will have to research extensively on new peripheries when the existing ones in your portfolio have fulfilled their growth potential.

Based on your preferred strategy, your eventual crypto portfolio will constitute of a number of different coins. Keep in mind that you will need a reasonable amount of time and effort to maintain whichever chosen strategy. Be very careful about investing in too many altcoins that you cannot keep track of your investments.

Personally, I use both Buy-And-Hold and Core-And-Peripheries strategies. At any point in time, I maintain at least 50% long positions in three to four altcoins. I trade the remainder coins and another three to four altcoins as peripheries to grow my stack of Ethereum. Lastly, I make it a point to cash out on Ethereum at strategic intervals so as to get cash positions to diversify into other markets or to buy back in during the dips.

Chapter Summary

For any form of investment, you start by determining your risk capital, which is the capital you can afford to lose. This is done by assessing your availability of excess cash and your personal risk appetite to see how much leftover you want to spend on investments.

Next, you define your investing guidelines and your goal of investing and choose the most appropriate strategy that suits your time and resource availability. This is necessary as you have to devote a certain amount of time to research and monitor your investments in order to minimise your risk.

Investing and trading can be rather similar in the cryptocurrency market. Investing takes on a relatively longer term outlook whereas trading is more short-term and capitalises on making multiple smaller profits.

However, the shorter market cycles and the greater magnitude of price movements in the market makes it easy for anyone to switch between investing and trading. As such, your "long-term" investment may last only a year or two as market cycles are shorter. Your "short-term" trades may also end up as long-term holdings because you might have taken sufficient profits when prices climb upwards quickly.

There is no best strategy out there and I believe it is about experimenting with what works best for you. In the following chapters, I will introduce several techniques so that you can time your entries, and more importantly, make your exits.

Pay attention to the qualitative factors in Chapter 4 for longer term investments while the trading guidelines in Chapter 5 would be more applicable for shorter term investments. Nonetheless, I think that they should all go hand in hand.

Chapter 4
Building Your Personalised Crypto Portfolio
How can we curate 'cryptoassets' for a mid-term to long-term investment period?

I advocate for a longer term investment in cryptocurrencies as I believe most people have not yet grasped the concept of blockchain and DLT, much less bought into cryptocurrencies. I believe that the market has yet to realise the true price value of cryptocurrencies and it would be a profitable investment in a few years, assuming you invest in the right coins.

Just like the many failed Internet companies in the DotCom bubble, I believe most cryptocurrencies today will not survive in the long run. Hence, this section introduces a way to pick out cryptocurrencies with good fundamentals. The obvious choice in the next one to two years will definitely be Bitcoin and Ethereum. After all, you need either of them to get access to the rest of the cryptocurrency market.

Beyond these two main cryptocurrencies, we have to properly assess the altcoins by examining their White Papers, their websites, and any other available channels. Just like any other investments, it is only wise if we do the due diligence before putting down our money.

Given the relatively short cryptocurrency market cycles, my definition of a mid to long-term investment is somewhere between two to five years. I would define short-term trades to last anything from a week to a few months.

Evaluating The Fundamentals

i. Functional purpose – Why blockchain?

The first thing you will encounter on a cryptocurrency's website or its White Paper will be an introduction and overview of the coin and what it does. Usually, there is a problem or a gap in the industry that the cryptocurrency seeks to address by applying blockchain technology.

It might sound extremely complicated but the common trend amongst all cryptocurrencies is that they are creating a decentralised system to mediate transactions. The difference amongst them is the type of transactions that they are mediating, and how they are addressing the limitations of blockchain technology. For example, it could be machine-to-machine transactions for an Internet-of-Things (IOT) cryptocurrency, user-to-user transactions of money or files, or user-to-organisation transactions of sensitive data.

The important question to ask is whether there is a need for the platform and its transactions to be on a distributed ledger. What is the significant advantage afforded by the DLT? By evaluating this question critically, you should be able to eliminate a lot of coins that are either scams or riding on the blockchain hype.

ii. Business model – Is it sustainable?

A business aims to make profits by earning enough revenue to cover their business costs. These profits go to stakeholders who have equity in the company.

Cryptocurrencies are run by a company but they aim to create a decentralised platform. Hence, the priority in evaluating the business model of a cryptocurrency should be whether it is sustainable, rather than whether it is profitable.

Think of the stakeholders in the ecosystem — the developers, the miners, the users, the partners. Where are the costs of the business incurred? Where does the "revenue" come from and to whom does it goes to? Will the recipients of the money continue to put back and contribute to the sustainability of the ecosystem?

For example, if Bitcoin is a monetary system, the cost of running this system are incurred by the mining expenses and the software development expenses. So how are the miners and the developers paid? When users buy Bitcoin and use Bitcoin, there is outflow of money, which will go to the miners. There appears to be a simple, sustainable flow of money for now.

What I am illustrating here is not whether these people are correct in the way they assign a value to Bitcoin. Instead, the above system is an example of a sustainable model. Contrast that with Bitconnect, a cryptocurrency that has been outrightly a scam.

The promise of Bitconnect was that users simply needed to hold on to these tokens and they would accumulate interest in Bitconnect tokens. They were also rewarded with tokens if they successfully referred more users. As such, its price should increase perpetually, and if everyone holds without using it, the value of the coins would be hyper-inflated and it would become even more expensive to use the coins, which was clearly unsustainable. Many people were misled into buying early, hoping to grow their money faster. They were oblivious to the economics of the coins.

The Bitconnect model proved unsustainable as the inflow of the money was heavier than the outflow. Owners have no incentive to use the tokens. Once a quick and heavy outflow was triggered, prices would plummet, and it happened when Bitconnect was issued a cease-and-desist letter in January 2018[14]. Early investors escaped unscathed and profitable in fact, while the ones who bought in later were left with worthless Bitconnect tokens.

To a certain extent, most cryptocurrencies today behave similarly as there are a large number of holders who are holding for the long run until it is widely adopted. They are also likely to be holding it

---

[14] Bitconnect's price went from mere dollars to over US$400 in its heydays, which was during the bull market in December 2017, and later dropped over 90% in a day when the cease-and-desist was official.

until they can cash out for significant profits, and hence the bubble-like price patterns when they sell their coins.

Hence, it is crucial to assess whether the economics of the cryptocurrency makes sense. That is to say, assuming that the cryptocurrency is eventually adopted widely, how would users consume their tokens and will the usage cycle be sustainable?

iii. Competition – Will it emerge victorious?

There are so many cryptocurrencies in the market that are trying to resolve the same problem with a decentralised token. How do you compare across competing cryptocurrencies? Furthermore, there are likely to be existing centralised solutions which compete for the attention and usage of these potential users. Thus, we have to look at competition not just between cryptocurrencies but also against competing applications.

For example, Basic Attention Token (BAT) is a cryptocurrency that seeks to change the way that people consume media and the way that advertisers target consumers. The BAT tokens are used to measure, reward, and price the engagement levels of different advertisements on their exclusive browser (Brave).

The crux of the change lies in users adopting a different web browser called Brave. In this instance, the competition involves a behavioural change for consumers to move away from their habit of using their preferred Safari or Chrome web browsers. This is besides the competition against other cryptocurrencies that aims to decentralise the system of advertising.

Likewise, cryptocurrencies that serve monetary or store-of-value functions are trying to induce a behavioural and ideological change in people's perception of money and assets. They have to convince people that digital money and digital assets are better than traditional ones for whatever reasons.

By looking at the competition, we can better assess the barriers of change and then consider the likelihood of resolving these challenges.

If you are looking to diversify your crypto portfolio, try not to invest in multiple coins that are tackling the same problem. Instead assess the likelihood that a cryptocurrency can edge over its competitors, and look towards diversifying into different industries and applications of DLT.

iv. Internal stakeholders - Who will make it happen?

Besides the product and its attributes, the development team is one of the most important factors to assess. After all, it is the team that puts together the White Paper and execute upon the business.

Then there are the partners who can contribute to the team's success by supporting with technical expertise, growing the team's network, or providing industrial applications. Information about the team and partners are usually found towards the back of the White Paper or the website.

You should dig deep into the credentials and the legitimacy of these people, which can be done by cross-referencing their personal websites with their LinkedIn and social media profiles. Most of the time, the founders and key developers are notable and respectable figures in the cryptocurrency space and you should easily find mentions of them online.

When investigating the type of partners that a cryptocurrency team has acquired, consider the relevance of their business and their expertise. Some cryptocurrencies may employ famous influencers and celebrities to endorse the product but have little impact on eventual adoption. We want to find a legitimate team with key strategic partners who can bring value to the team and increase the likelihood of success and adoption.

v. Strategic timeline – Is there continuous development?

The roadmap to development, implementation, and adoption has to be strategic and reasonable. This is where you assess the milestones for a cryptocurrency so that you can check back and see if your investment is on track.

One thing to take note is that development on the blockchain and DLT tends to be more complicated and may take a longer time than expected. This is because an implementation on a distributed ledger is extremely difficult to reverse once it is distributed to everyone. Development teams usually go through multiple rounds of extensive testing and auditing before making an official beta release. The actual launch will usually be even later.

Hence, delays in the development pipeline and launches are not unusual. Instead, you could consider how the team is addressing these delays. As long as they are moving forward towards the goal steadily and communicating their progress transparently, it is a sign that the cryptocurrency is legit.

vi. Community – How is the ground-level support?

The size and strength of the community can drive the adoption of the cryptocurrency. Although this does not directly affect the development of the product or the team, having active user feedback and suggestions would help push the cryptocurrency forward.

Some communities even initiate their own features and projects built on top of the cryptocurrency. For example, communities are known to take on projects to integrate their favourite coins on different hardware wallets. They have also built applications like payment gateways for e-commerce stores to accept their favourite cryptocurrencies. Popular channels to find these communities are Reddit, Telegram, Discord, and Slack.

vii. Market cap and volume – What do the numbers say?

The market capitalisation (cap) is often used to estimate the worth of a cryptocurrency, and is determined by the last transacted price of a coin multiplied by its circulating supply. The market volume, on the other hand, indicates the trading activity of the cryptocurrency on a given day.

The problem with the market cap is that a cryptocurrency's worth is estimated using its circulating supply, which is a very inaccurate measure. Many cryptocurrencies withhold their supply of coins until further stages of development and these are not accounted for in the market cap. Nonetheless, the circulating supply can be a useful metric to gauge the type of ecosystem planned and how scarce a coin aims to be.

Changes in the market cap can also give us a broad overview of sentiments in the cryptocurrency market, assuming the supply of coins and the total number of different cryptocurrencies do not increase too quickly. We can contrast these sentiments with the market volume of the coin and how active the recent trades have been. We can also use sentiment analysis and Google Trends to support our findings.

The key takeaway is that we have to evaluate cryptocurrencies in its entirety and not base our decision solely on one or two measures.

Quantitative Evaluation of Fundamentals

Putting the fundamentals together, we can assign weights to the above mentioned factors to have a quantitative way to compare between cryptocurrencies. In the following example, feel free to modify the factors on the left column and their respective weights.

Take note, you should compare cryptocurrencies that are trying to serve the same function and not a currency-type token against a security-type token. For example, you can compare Bitcoin (BTC), with Bitcoin Cash (BCH), Litecoin (LTC), and Zcash (ZEC) to assess which ones make a better currency-type of coin.

There could also be frequent changes in these factors so you should constantly reevaluate these measures.

		Coin A	Sub-Total (A)	Coin B	Sub-Total (B)
	Weight				
People					
Team	0.1	4	0.4	3	0.3
Partnership	0.1	2	0.2	5	0.5
Community	0.1	4	0.4	5	0.5
Product			0		0
Function(s)	0.1	5	0.5	4	0.4
Concept	0.1	4	0.4	5	0.5
Business Model	0.1	2	0.2	4	0.4
USP/Value	0.1	2	0.2	4	0.4
Process			0		0
PR/Publicity	0.05	5	0.25	2	0.1
On Schedule	0.05	2	0.1	1	0.05
Development Plan	0.1	3	0.3	1	0.1
Market Environment			0		0
Market Cap	0.025	5	0.125	3	0.075
Market Volume	0.025	5	0.125	3	0.075
Competition	0.05	2	0.1	3	0.15
Total Score	1		3.3		3.55

Table 2. Comparison of two cryptocurrencies, A and B.

An Alternative Cryptocurrency Taxonomy

Keeping in mind the typical categorisation of currency, securities, and utility tokens, I propose an alternative way to look at cryptoassets — **currency, store of value, protocol improvement, coin-as-a-service, and utility tokens**. These categories are not mutually exclusive and a cryptocurrency can span across multiple categories.

Category	Function	Examples
Currency	Similar to money, it aims to create a digital and decentralised form of currency.	BTC, BCH, LTC, MNR, NANO, DASH
Store Of Value	Similar to assets, it is an alternative way to store monetary value.	DGD, USDT, Stable Coins
Protocol Improvement	It addresses limitations in the current system so that blockchain and DLT can improve altogether.	ZEC, MNR, IOTA
Coin-As-A-Service	It allows anyone to create their own crypto tokens more easily.	ETH, NEO, WAVES, ARK
Utility Token	It transforms existing services into a decentralised and tokenised economy.	BNB. ZRX, AUG, SIA, BAT, GNT

Table 3. Summary of cryptocurrency categories.

By classifying cryptocurrencies this way, I have grouped them based on their associated functions and each category poses a similar set of risks. For example, coins in the currency category aim to be an alternative to fiat money and they face a similar set of challenges in getting adoption and regulatory risks.

Hence, if you are looking to diversify, you should be looking at buying cryptocurrencies across different categories. Classifying your tokens across these categories will also help you to monitor and evaluate competing coins in the same category.

i. Currency – A standardised mode-of-payment

The first category comprises of tokens that function as a form of payment currency. They were designed to be a universal digital currency that users can exchange with one another, and aims to be a standardised currency used across the globe.

In order for any currency to work, they have to be stable, accepted, and fungible. Stability refers to how the value of a coin remains relatively constant over time. Acceptability refers to how widely accepted and how recognised its price value is. Fungibility refers to how interchangeable one coin is with another.

Cryptocurrencies today are volatile, not commonly accepted, and relatively fungible. It would be hard to use Bitcoin to buy something today if its value were to be halved the next day. Price volatility and acceptability will take a while to normalise. As such, cryptocurrencies may not be better than fiat currencies today.

Furthermore, Bitcoin as a universal currency is not exactly fungible. People across different countries value cryptocurrencies differently. For example, to exchange for a Bitcoin, people in Zimbabwe and Venezuela have to pay about 30% more of their fiat currency to exchange for the same Bitcoin. This is partly because the value of their fiat currency is deflating rapidly while the demand for Bitcoin is extremely high. The demand, the accessibility, and the regulations of cryptocurrencies differ vastly across the world, which why it is still not fungible today.

Perhaps, the issue is that cryptocurrency is still in its infancy today. It is not entirely scalable, usable, or accepted by a global pool of users, yet. Protocols are still being tested, regulations are being worked out, and more educational materials are needed to teach the masses the technical know-how to use cryptocurrency safely and reliably.

Nonetheless, Bitcoin has been proven conceptually and I believe that it is only a matter of time before these limitations will be resolved and cryptocurrencies will be widely accepted.

ii. Store Of Value – An alternative asset

Although cryptocurrencies may not be useful payment currencies yet, they are a relatively viable store of value. Assets like art, gold, commodities are a reasonable store of value because they are scarce and there is a globally recognised market value. Similarly, cryptocurrencies are scarce and most people recognise that there is some utility value although they cannot quantify whether it is currently under or overvalued. Nonetheless, the fact that there is some form of value makes it a plausible asset.

If we were to base Bitcoin solely on its utility of retaining value, of being distributed, decentralised, secure, and immutable, it already functions well as a store of value. It might even be better than art or properties because it is divisible and more liquid. If you had acquired any of the store-of-value cryptocurrencies early on, their market value would also have appreciated significantly and your investment would still be positive even in a bear market.

On another hand, there are also some cryptocurrencies that peg each coin to a physical dollar or an ounce of gold, which they store in their reserves. These assets-backed cryptocurrencies are similar to securities in a sense and you will have to trust these companies to store the reserve assets. Although it is somewhat centralised, this form of cryptocurrency would help to win over investors who are more familiar with traditional investments.

Tether (USDT) and the likes of cryptocurrencies that are pegged to physical assets are becoming increasingly common and recognised. There is a sub-category that we call "Stable Coins" [15] where the supplies of these coins float so that their price value remains stable and do not fluctuate along with the rest of the market. Nonetheless, this entire category of cryptocurrencies run the risk of being classified as securities, with strict rules being implemented in future.

---

[15] Stable coins are centralised and an organisation is responsible for ensuring the integrity of their system, so it brings about issues as to whether the organisation is trustable.

iii. Protocol Improvement – Resolve existing limitations

Cryptocurrencies in this category aim to improve on the existing blockchain infrastructure and typically address certain limitations in the current technology like interoperability, anonymity, and scalability.

Interoperability refers to how different coins can coexist by having a common programming language so that they can operate with one another. Anonymity refers to the extent that the senders and the receivers of the coins can be tracked and monitored. Scalability refers to the capacity of the infrastructure to cope with increased number of users and transactions.

When the cryptocurrency bull run and when ICOs were extremely popular towards the end of 2017, the increased volume on the Bitcoin and Ethereum network led to slow transaction rates. Transaction fees were also extremely high as they were measured in coins, so the fees increase rapidly along with the prices of the coins. Today, protocols are still being experimented to increase the transaction rates and minimise transaction fees. The Lightning Network for Bitcoin and Sharding for Ethereum are proposed solutions to make them more scalable.

Other cryptocurrencies are devising new methods of DLT that are not blockchain in structure. For example, the Directed Acyclic Graph (DAG) type of altcoins proposes for transactions to be stored in a neural-like structure instead of a blockchain. For now, all these protocol-improvement coins are still a work in progress but they are definitely at the forefront of "value creation" in contributing towards DLT.

iv. Coin-as-a-service (CAAS) – Make token creation accessible

As DLT gradually displaces traditional systems, some cryptocurrencies believe in making it easier for users to create their own tokens. Picture how Wordpress allows anyone to create their own website using templates and HTML (hypertext markup language), and how Shopify allows a layman to create their own e-commerce store. CAAS tokens aim to democratise the creation of tokenised systems.

Ethereum's programming language, Solidity, was designed with a simpler programming language than Bitcoin to make it easier for programmers to pick up. Many other CAAS cryptocurrencies are creating token frameworks based on existing popular programming languages like CSS, Java, and Python. Their goal is to encourage more software developers to join in the programming of blockchain systems.

There are also tokens like ARK and OST that are deploying user-friendly interfaces so that an individual or a business without programming expertise can initiate their own blockchain tokens on their systems.

Ethereum is probably the most successful example to date as it has allowed many other cryptocurrencies to be created with the ERC20 token standard and inadvertently led to the rise of ICOs. However, for CAAS-type tokens to work and become valuable, they have to be able to capture a critical mass of users and prove a solid use case, like smart contracts.

There is also an underlying assumption that blockchain services will become the norm in future such that organisations would want to create their own tokens. Most retail investors are unlikely to create their own blockchain tokens so these tokens would not exactly be functional for them.

v. Utility Tokens – Implement widespread blockchain usage

Most cryptocurrencies today are likely to be a utility token. Utility-type cryptocurrencies are tokens you hold so that you can exchange for the blockchain-based services and products offered by that company. It does not represent an equity stake but merely some guarantee of a service in exchange for these tokens.

Utility tokens aim to put existing transactional systems onto the blockchain, whether it is to transform the supply chain, store customer data, or facilitate commerce activities. The major argument is whether there is a need for there to be tokens at all, especially when existing systems today function well without tokens. How do the upsides of security, immutability, and decentralisation weigh against the many limitations of DLT today?

The main difference between buying these utility tokens before the system is up and running is that you get a discounted rate in the services. That is to say, when you buy the tokens at current prices and they becomes more expensive in future, you will have capital appreciation and you will be able to consume more of the same service with the tokens you hold. Hence, cryptocurrencies are speculative in that sense because you can put your bets on the survivability of a token and hope to sell them to users in future.

It then brings us to the question as to whether the capital gains you are expecting outweighs the risk of investing and holding these tokens. That is why qualitative research plays an important role in mitigating your risks.

The Myth Of Diversification

The objective of learning how to analyse and classify cryptocurrencies is so that you can build a diversified portfolio. Diversification reduces the risk of your entire investment going to zero, which may happen if you put all your eggs into one basket and that basket drops.

However, how many baskets can you afford to hold at any one time? If you overly diversify, you end up spreading yourself too thin. Your investment may not make a significant return on investments, or you might end up with bad eggs because you do not pay enough attention to picking out only the good ones.

Investment is a personal journey and I think that the right array of cryptocurrencies differ for everyone. Start with three or four cryptocurrencies and gradually build upon the diversity of your portfolio. When you find that you cannot cope with the number of cryptocurrencies in your portfolio any further, cut the number by half and focus on the ones that you truly believe in.

A healthy portfolio should not only be measured by its quantitative performance but also by how much physical and mental resources you have to spend in order to achieve those results.

Chapter Summary

The allure of cryptocurrency is its possibility to serve a variety of functions and industries and it disrupts the fundamental way that users transact with one another. The objective of this chapter is to develop your own framework to assess the functions and qualitative factors of cryptocurrencies so as to mitigate your risk and to create a diversified portfolio.

If we were to liken the onset of cryptocurrencies with the Internet revolution, most crypto companies today will not see it to the end so it boils down to picking the winners. Diversification helps to spread out your risk and increase the likelihood of you holding the cryptocurrencies that will be eventually be adopted.

In my investment journey, I have learnt that we can try to be objective and rational in our decisions but the market is irrational and built upon speculation. In the short term, altcoins with "poor" fundamentals may rise instead because of the news and hype.

I often question my strategy because speculating seems to be far more effective than being logical. These are the times when I feel a sense of FOMO (Fear Of Missing Out) and what-ifs when I see my portfolio stagnating while some random cryptocurrency shoots up.

If you do face this experience, remember that you are looking at things with a hindsight bias. Go back to the beginning of this book section and remind yourself of your investment goals. If you are looking at a long-term investment, you must have a basis for selecting cryptocurrencies, and short-term fluctuations should not be your concern. If you are looking at making quick gains, then question your strategy. For example, would a speculative, sentiment-based analysis work better for short-term trading?

In the following chapters, I will introduce trading tactics and address some of these psychological factors so that you can be prepared for the cryptocurrency market.

Chapter 5
Thriving In The Wild Wild West
How can we time our trades and maximise our returns?

Investing-Specific Tactics

The goal of investing is to generate profits over an extended period of time. In the cryptocurrency market, that would mean ignoring the short-term fluctuations and focusing on the long-term price appreciation.

Assuming that the cryptocurrency market is still in its infancy, any purchase price now is a good price if you pick the right cryptocurrency. As such, most of your attention should be focused on the fundamentals, and the following two tactics can help minimise your investment risk.

i. Dollar Cost Averaging (DCA)

Given the long-term landscape of investing, you cannot be absolutely sure whether you are currently entering at a low or high point. As such, you can make use of DCA to make entries at multiple price points so as to get an average price of entry.

You can utilise DCA in two ways. The first is to make regular time-based entries. For example, you can dedicate a fraction of your monthly income to buy cryptocurrencies at the end of each month. Over the course of a year, the price of your entry into cryptocurrencies would have been averaged out.

The second way is to make regular price-interval-based entries. For example, as the price of a cryptocurrency dips rapidly, you make regular entries at every 20% drop in price. If you bought at $100, the next price to buy is $80, then $64, then $51.

For people who are familiar with applying DCA in other types of investments, do note that you should be buying at larger intervals when you DCA in the cryptocurrency market i.e. 20% intervals versus 5% intervals. This is to account for the extreme volatility of cryptocurrency as prices can fluctuate more than 100% in a day.

> *"The best time to invest was yesterday, the second best time is now." – Unknown.*

ii. Diversify your cryptocurrencies

As mentioned earlier, diversifying your portfolio spreads out your risk. You place your bets in a handful of coins instead of just one. The caveat to diversification is that you will need extra time and effort to monitor and research the altcoins properly.

Given that there is too much (mis)information out there, it is sometimes better to work with what you have and what you know. It may be wiser and less risky to just focus on the cryptocurrencies that you have thoroughly researched on.

For a long-term investment in cryptocurrencies, you can ignore the short-term price fluctuations. Dedicate your resources to research and you can get by with a simple DCA and diversification strategy.

Trading-Specific Tactics

The goal of trading is to generate short-term profits with more frequent buying and selling of cryptocurrencies. As such, trading would demand more time and effort, and your goal is to outperform the buy-and-hold investing strategy in the short run.

The following tips will be very useful if you are planning to use the "Shooting To The Moon With Alts" or "Core And Peripheries" strategies.

i. DCA your entries and exits

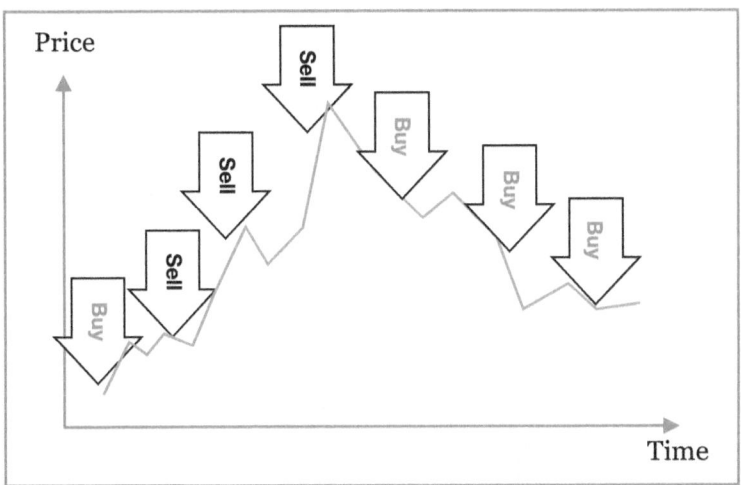

Diagram 4. Dollar cost average – average your buys and sells.

As mentioned earlier, this is a common tactic used by traders to average their buys and sells. It can be applied when you are buying the dips as the market declines or selling as the market rises.

For example, say a coin drops from $100 to $80 when you decide to make your first purchase. Instead of putting in a lump sum investment at $80, you can put in a third of the money. When it drops to $70, you put in another third, and if it drops further to $60, you put in the remaining amount. This way, your entry price would have been averaged down to $70.

Similarly, when the market moves upwards and you are looking to sell, you can average your exit prices. Hence, people usually apply DCA to sell during a bullish trend or to buy during a bearish market.

ii. Put trailing stop losses

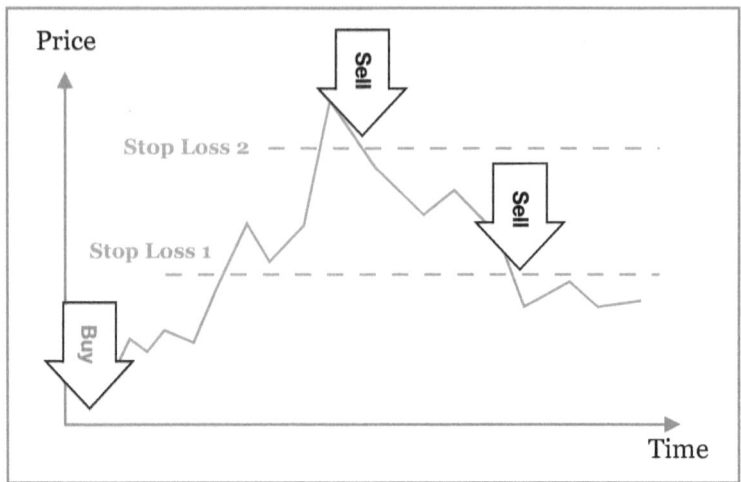

Diagram 5. Trailing stop losses.

When prices of a cryptocurrency keep going up, it is tempting to keep holding to watch your portfolio rise. However, with the wild fluctuations in cryptocurrency prices, your portfolio can fall back down all the way within a day. As such, when prices hit your desired target levels, it is advisable to sell a portion of it, and set a trailing stop loss on the remainder.

For example, if a coin rises from $1 to your target of $2, you sell some of it at $2 and set a stop loss on the remainder. If you put a trailing stop loss at $1.80, you sell a portion if it drops back down below $1.80. If prices continue to go upwards to $3 or $5, you adjust your trailing stop loss upwards.

In the diagram above, the first stop loss level was not met so there was no need to sell. Then, you raise your stop loss level as prices keep increasing. When the price reversed at the peak and hit the second raised stop loss, that is when you should sell a portion. If prices continue upwards, you raise the stop loss level again. In this case, prices went back down below the first stop loss level, which is when you should sell another portion.

Conceptually, putting stop losses and sticking to it ensures that you take profits. If prices go southwards, it also minimises your exposure to risk. The challenge comes in finding the right portion of coins to cash out when your stop loss levels are met. For a start, you can experiment with selling 20% of your portfolio and adjust this ratio thereafter.

iii. Be late to the party

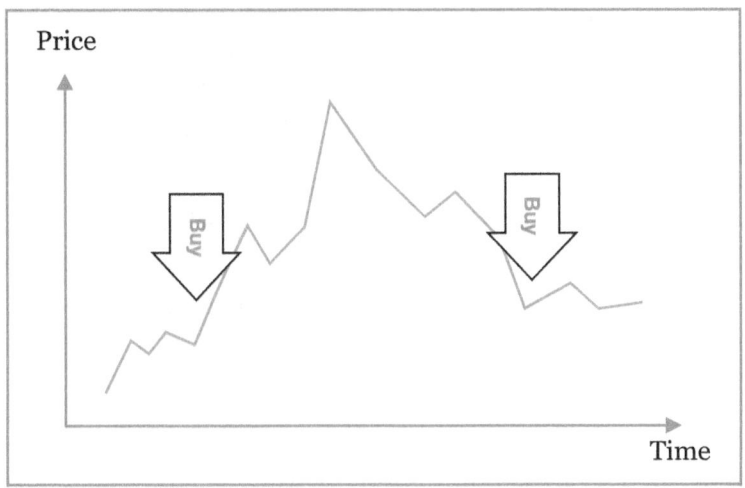

Diagram 6. Enter when there is a clear upwards trend or after a market correction.

Prices of cryptocurrencies can surge by a few hundred percent in a day, especially when there are major news or rumours. Many newcomers may experience FOMO (Fear of Missing Out) and jump into the market rashly. That can be a costly mistake.

The rise of Ripple (XRP) in December 2017 was a fine example. With the media reporting that Ripple can replace traditional banking and remittance industries, speculators drove the price of XRP from around $0.20 to over $3.50 in a month. The late investors who wanted to catch the bandwagon to $5 or even $10 suffered as Ripple went back down.

You should make your entries when prices are clearly going upwards or reversing from a bottom. The concept of being late to the party is that you should not let the FOMO get to you. To be confident of the upwards or reversal trend, you will definitely have to use the technical analyses. Otherwise, it would be a complete guess if you were to just look blindly at the chart.

In the case of Ripple, technical indicators have indicated signs of being overbought, which means that it may be better to wait for a market correction to enter. This will also minimise your risk of entering at the most expensive prices.

Market corrections are generally easier to spot than a reversal or upwards trend, and we should still rely on technical indicators to catch the bottom of the correction.

Hence, whenever you feel inclined to jump into the market or if you are unsure about the market sentiments, it is better to stay out of the market. Look for the next opportunity instead because you do not have to play every hand dealt to you.

You probably can tell by now that technical analyses play a crucial role in trading. That is why we cannot take any of these trading advice at surface level, and should not rely solely on one tactic to trade the market.

iv. Leave the party early

Once the price has hit your target level, you can either set stop loss levels or you can afford to leave the party entirely and close all your positions. Even if the party decides to continue on and prices keep going upwards, try not to look at all the potential gains that you are missing out on if you had held on.

Instead, you can spend the effort to evaluate your options and decide on the next hand to play. You have now consolidated on your cash positions, which allows you to make the next entry into another cryptocurrency or to diversify your portfolio into traditional investments.

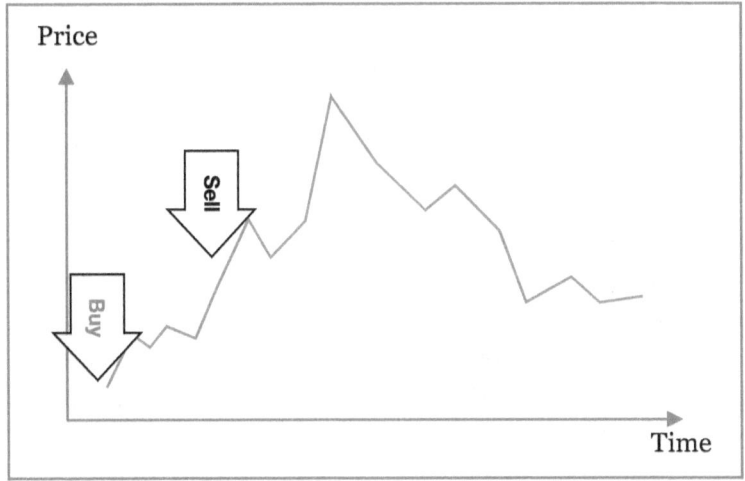

Diagram 7. Sell before prices peak out.

If prices do drop and hit your stop loss level, you should also be disciplined about exiting the market. Consolidate your cash positions, reevaluate your trading strategies, and work on your next trade. The most important takeaway is to assess the strategy that you have used and work on improving it

A Preview Of Technical Analysis

Technical analysis (TA) is a way to forecast price movements in the market based on previous price charts of different assets. Traders use technical indicators like chart patterns, support and resistance levels, trend lines, and other complex mathematical formulae to make educated guesses as to where the price of an asset is headed next.

There are traders who have been profitable using just one technical indicator, a variety of them, or even none. That is because indicators are just tools and you have to understand how these tools work, in order to use them effectively. It is advisable to skip technicals if you are unfamiliar with them and focus on the fundamentals instead.

Some people argue that TA is using the past to predict the future and it may well be a form of confirmation bias. It is founded on the belief that people behave and react in a similar way to price movements in the market and hence it is possible to predict the likely outcome based on historical trends. Furthermore, the speculative nature of the crypto market makes it possible to be profitable just by following market sentiments.

For me, I use TA to supplement my qualitative evaluations so that I take profits at opportunistic moments and buy back in on the market corrections. In the long run, my goal is to grow and accumulate my cryptocurrency holdings even if they somehow become worthless. I see it as a process to learn the technicals and I will share briefly on two indicators and the basis behind them.

i. Support and Resistance Levels

Support levels are price levels where there are a lot of buy orders placed for an asset at a particular price. It is a price level where a lot of investors believe that the asset is worth. Hence, when prices of drop to these support zones, many buy orders are automatically triggered and prices do not seem to drop any further.

Resistance level is the exact opposite where a lot of sell orders are placed at a price level such that an upwards moving price trend will find it difficult to go beyond that price as there are many sell orders waiting to be filled.

To find the support and resistance levels, you should find the common turning points on the chart over a time period rather than in one instance. Support levels are price zones that you can buy with a little more confidence while resistance levels are price zones that you should take some profits.

What is more useful about finding these levels is looking for breakouts beyond these support or resistance zones. When the support level is broken, it means that the sell orders now outweigh the previously strong buy orders and prices are likely to plummet lower to the next support level. Similarly, when a resistance level is broken, it means that the buy orders have exceeded the sell orders and we are heading upwards to the next resistance zone.

A resistance level that was broken will become a support level when prices drop back. When a support level is broken and the price goes lower, the same level will become a resistance level when the price rises back. Hence, if you have a recorded all the major support and resistance levels on a price chart, they will become price bands for you to buy and sell.

ii. Moving Averages (MA)

Moving averages are the average of price movements across a period of time. There is the simple moving average (SMA) and the exponential moving average (EMA). The number before the MA indicates the time period. For example, 9SMA represents the nine most recent daily closing prices of an asset.

A moving average is marked by a line that indicates the up and down movement of the average daily closing price.

By plotting a short-term MA with a mid-term MA, e.g. 9SMA with 25SMA, you can see which price trend is stronger. If the shorter period SMA crosses above the longer period SMA, e.g. 9MA >

25MA, or 50MA >200MA, it signals a bullish trend in the short run.

Conversely, if the bigger number MA line is above the smaller number MA line, it means that the short-term sentiments are weaker than the long-term sentiments. This signals a downwards bearish trend in the short term. If you are looking at a longer-term investment, you chart the 50MA against the 200MA rather than the 9MA against the 25MA.

The point of comparing two different MA is to assess which time-averaged price is stronger and thus suggests whether prices are heading upwards or downwards. This brings us to MACD (Moving Average Convergence Divergence) indicator, which tracks the movement of the two MA lines towards one another or away from one another and is often used to confirm a price trend.

For cryptocurrencies, the EMA is more suitable as the exponentially weighted average better accounts for the rapidly changing prices in a volatile market.

Do note that MA, in general, are lagging indicators, which means that the trend has already been forming before it can be seen on the charts. Hence, traders usually use MA as a confirmation signal rather than a signal to act upon.

Case Study: IOTA (MIOTA)

Fundamentals

IOTA is a non-blockchain cryptocurrency token. It was designed as a Internet-Of-Things token and promises several advantages over traditional blockchain systems:

1. More Scalable: Transaction speeds are not restricted by blocks and block times, and will theoretically get faster as more users adopt the system.

2. Quantum-Proof: One criticism of Proof-of-Work mining is that quantum computers can make them obsolete[16]; IOTA's ternary design was employed with quantum computing in mind.

3. Team and Partnerships: IOTA has forged notable partnerships with Bosch, Volkswagen, and Fujitsu for various applications. Its team is constantly expanding although there are concerns on the attitude and work ethics of the founders.

As a store-of-value or payment-type currency, IOTA is already functional. This is further complemented by its mobile wallet. IOTA also utilises a Directed Acyclic Graph design that is an alternative protocol to the blockchain. Currently, its data marketplace and smart contracts function are still in the works and would take at least another year before it can be implemented.

Assuming you have gone through all the potential upsides and downsides and decided to put some money into IOTA, now let us look at the technicals to determine a good entry and exit point.

Technicals

IOTA is currently (August 2018) at the red colour mark of around $0.72. It was trading around $0.40 in October 2017 and shot to its peak of over $5 in December 2017.

---

[16] Quantum computers are super powerful computers that can plug in hashes so quickly, which makes currently mining processes useless.

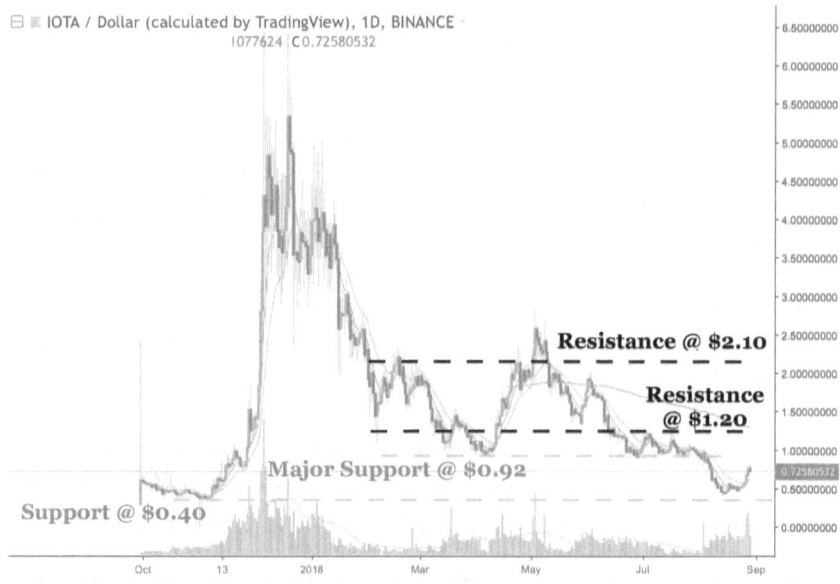

Diagram 8. IOTA Price Chart, Daily Candle, from Tradingview.

The support level of around $0.40 was established early on in 2017, but has since been broken. When the bear market started (reversed from over $5), the $0.92 level was a major support level that has not been broken from March 2018 till August 2018.

Hence, the break below $0.92 was a good opportunity to capture the move to the next support zone ($0.40). Alternatively, when prices drop close to the $0.40 level, it was a good entry point.

The next target would be an upside move to $0.92 where the previous support level will become an important resistance level. Whether the price is more likely to head towards $0.92 or back down to $0.40, you will have to look more closely at the Weekly and Hourly charts, and also use the smaller EMAs (blue and green lines) that cannot really be seen in this picture.

Following which, the next resistance level to look out for is around $1.20, and then $2.10. However, the candles will most likely have to break above the 200EMA mark (purple line) for these upside targets to become more plausible.

Taking Profits And Reevaluating Trades

Although I am still in the process of learning and experimenting with the technical indicators, knowing how to read the charts gives me an extra bit of confidence in executing my buy and sell orders. For a mid-term trade, I find it necessary to take profits or close losing positions and look for the next opportunity. Overall, my portfolio consists mainly of long-term positions and only a portion of it is dedicated to experimenting with mid-term trades.

When my first investment in Ethereum grew, I made the mistake of diversifying into altcoins that I did not research much about. As a result, my total quantity of ETH dropped even though it may only be a portion of it. The altcoins were eventually worthless.

Having learnt to assess the fundamentals, I decided to venture into altcoins again in the next boom and made sure to do my homework to understand the cryptocurrency, its team, and its development. However, I bought in at the highs and did not take profits when the altcoins appreciated against Ethereum. I broke even on most altcoins while I currently hold long-term positions in some of them.

Had I just stuck with holding Ethereum, I would have been in a profit but I would not have learnt many of these lessons. Thus, I see this constant reevaluation of investing strategies as a learning process.

Learn to choose the right coins if you plan to invest in cryptocurrencies for the long term. On another hand, if you want to trade cryptocurrencies, you have to learn to take profits and constantly evaluate your strategies.

Chapter Summary

The objective of this chapter is to introduce you to several techniques that you can apply for your investment. If you are looking to invest for a longer term, using fundamentals alone may suffice while DCA reduces your risk of buying at an extreme high.

What is your goal of investing? Do you want to build a passive stream of income, to accumulate wealth gradually, or to make a lump sum in a short time (sounds like gambling)?

After all, investing is about being profitable and if you are looking to take profits in the shorter term, you should definitely pick up some technical analyses. Some people say that fundamentals tell you what to buy while technicals tell you when to buy. Regardless of which strategy you adopt, remember that the more comprehensive your research, the lower your risk but the more time and energy required.

To summarise all the steps mentioned from Chapters 3 to 5:

1. Determine your risk profile.
2. Set aside a portion of your savings or income for cryptocurrency.
3. Determine your grounds rules of investing.
4. Set your goals for investing or trading.
5. Pick the coins to buy by assessing the fundamentals.
6. Enter the market opportunistically using technicals, or simply dollar cost average.
7. Exit the market strategically and periodically to get cash positions.
8. Consolidate positions and evaluate on your next trade.
9. You may skip Steps 7 to 9 if you are planning to buy and hold for long-term.

Chapter 6

Market Forces And Human Behaviour

What are the drivers of the crypto market and how can we capitalise on them?

Newcomers to the cryptocurrency market are often disadvantaged. They are up against people who have either started earlier at lower prices or professionals who have the technical knowledge from prior trading experience in stocks, forex, and options. This chapter is about the non-conventional and unique rules to the cryptocurrency market that many people do not know about.

The following tactics work because of the following factors that are unique to the cryptocurrency market: active 24/7 trading, market speculation, a large portion of holders, emotion-driven prices, and market manipulation. These tactics are unlikely to work outside of the cryptocurrency context.

Furthermore, as the cryptocurrency landscape is still evolving, some of these tactics may become obsolete in future. While this knowledge can give you an edge over others, do not just apply them blindly. It is important to understand why and how they work so that you can adapt your gameplay when some of these market forces change.

Playing In A 24/7 Global Market

The cryptocurrency is constantly active in every part of the world. It is a market that does not sleep. It is a market that is highly interconnected. An impact in Asia can have either a resonating effect or opposing effect in the Western part of the world.

This was apparent from September 2017's incident. What started as rumours between the Chinese authorities and domestic coin exchanges became a passed legislation – coin exchanges were disallowed from facilitating fiat-to-cryptocurrency trades. That is to say, it will be illegal for the coin exchange operators to facilitate such trades and for Chinese citizens to buy and sell cryptocurrencies with Chinese Yuan.

The regulatory news started in China but had a global impact as everyone feared that their governments will impose a similar regulation. Massive sell-offs of cryptocurrencies soon followed from around the world.

After weeks of plummeting prices, with greater selling pressure from the Eastern side of the world, the episode ended with a sudden surge of buy-ins, presumably from other parts of the world when prices hit a low.[17]

i. Differences in trading hours

In the September 2017, the optimal time to buy into the lows was between noon and afternoon in Asia. This was due to the higher sell volume from Asia relative to the buy volumes from around the world. Subsequently, when it was night time in Asia (and daytime in the West), prices would have recovered slightly as the buy volumes in the West outweighed the sell volume in the East. Coincidentally, when the market did an instant recovery and price

---

[17] Prices of Bitcoin and Ethereum were actually a lot lower on domestic Chinese exchanges than global coin exchanges as people were aggressively dumping their cryptocurrencies.

reversed rapidly, it was night time in Asia where there would have been less trading activity.

Between January 2018 to March 2018, the cryptocurrency market was also bearish. If you wanted to catch the lowest prices of the day, it will tend to be around 8—10 AM US time or around evening in Asian times. A possible explanation is that it was tax period in the US and hence there was greater selling pressure around the opening trading hours in the US.

If you are aware of the active trading hours and familiar with the difference in market sentiments across geographic regions, you will be able to enter and exit the market strategically. However, do note that such opportunities may not always be present.

ii. Arbitrage opportunities

The idea of arbitrage is to buy low on one exchange and sell higher on another exchange. To successfully arbitrage, you would need to hold accounts with a balance of BTC or ETH on multiple coin exchanges.

The rationale for arbitrage is that there is an asymmetry of news and information. One part of the world would have first reacted to certain pieces of news before another, which leads to more buy or sell orders in that particular region.

This leads to price disparities across different coin exchanges. The latency in information creates arbitrage opportunities that can last anything from minutes to hours, and prices can differ as much as 10-20% between the two coin exchanges.

Arbitrage must be executed almost simultaneously on both exchanges. If you are looking to sell off on an exchange, transfer it over to another, and then buy the coins back, the window of price difference might have already passed. You might end up incurring the withdrawal and transaction fees instead. Hence, you will need to have BTC or ETH in both exchanges to arbitrage, so storing of your coins on the exchanges is the risk to bear.

iii. Weekend consolidations

Trading activity tends to be higher on weekends than on weekdays. As the market operates 24/7, it is usually on weekends when the general crowd goes through the news and decide on the trades to make.

When market sentiments are neutral to poor, prices tend to be about 5% higher on weekdays than on weekends. From Mondays to Thursdays, prices will rise steadily until the weekend draws near. Following which, because of the FUD (fear, uncertainty, doubt) surrounding the market, prices will drop back on Saturdays and Sundays, to the levels at the start of the week.

However, if the general sentiments are positive, prices will tend to hold steady on weekends and might rise a further 5-10% when people make their trades. So the market really can go both ways depending on the general sentiments surrounding the cryptocurrency space.

You can make use of these small fluctuations to expand on your cryptocurrency holdings but do trade these small fluctuations with only a portion of your portfolio rather than your entire portfolio. Otherwise, any sudden changes in market conditions can see prices rising exponentially and you do not want to be out of the market then.

Hitching Alongside The Manipulators

Market manipulation and insider trading in the stock market is illegal. However, given the relative anonymity of cryptocurrency trades and the current lack of regulations, market manipulation is rampant in the cryptocurrency market.

Although there were never any hard evidence, most people who have been in the space long enough are aware that the market is heavily manipulated. All it takes is for someone with either an extensive amount of money or an extensive amount of Bitcoin holdings to influence the market. These people who are often referred to as 'whales' can influence a market trend or reversal simply by putting up a ginormous buy or sell order.

As small players, we have to consider the likelihood and consequences of the whales' actions. That is to say, by making guesses about the whales' next move and the impact of their trades, we will be more ready to deal with the prices changes and subsequently capitalise on those opportunities.

i. Think like the whales

The term 'whales' is used to describe people who hold a large quantity of a particular coin. They could be early adopters or the founding team of the cryptocurrency who bought the coins at really low prices or were paid for their work in coins. They could also be rich individuals or groups of people who pooled their finances together to accumulate a significant portion of the total supply. Institutional-level investment funds, for example, have the monetary resource to invest like whales.

Amongst the whales, there are those who truly believe in the cryptocurrency project and are holding the coins for the long term. Then, there are the ones who are in it solely for the speculation and the profits. Regardless of their intention, their eventual goal is to either use the coin when it is widely adopted or sell them at their desired price levels.

I find it useful to put myself in the shoes of the whales each time I am trying to catch a market high to sell or a market low to buy. If the market rises, I would question how long the momentum can keep going and how much I can sell so that the upward price movement will not be disrupted. As a whale, what is the ideal action for me to take?

Conversely, if I want to crash the market as a whale, I will think of finding a slowing momentum period and cashing out to cause a downward spiral. When prices drop to a new low, I will be able to buy back in at a bargain. As a whale, how can I time my actions with market news and sentiments so that the market can go lower?

Your expectation and anticipation of a whale's actions may not be very accurate but that is inconsequential. The useful aspect of thinking like whales is that going through these thoughts forces you to slow you down and not make an impulsive trade. It is when you take a step back to consider the possible reasons for the current price movement, will you then be able to respond appropriately to the market.

First, you think like whales. Then, you act like whales. Lastly, you remember that you are just a small fish in the big ocean.

ii. Use BTC price movement as an indicator

In order for most new entrants to join the cryptocurrency market, they have to either purchase Bitcoin or Ethereum, which they then trade for other cryptocurrencies. When they make their exits, they have to go through Bitcoin or Ethereum again. How can we use this knowledge to our advantage?

Imagine a super big player or institution looking to enter the cryptocurrency market, he will likely use technical analyses to plan his Bitcoin buy order. We are looking at orders upwards of hundreds of thousands of dollars, which when triggered will affect prices significantly. What we are looking out for here is where the support and resistance levels are, as mentioned earlier.

The trick here is that you do not have to run analyses on every single coin. The cryptocurrency market follows the price movement of Bitcoin very closely because it is the main cryptocurrency after all. This means that when the price of Bitcoin drops, the prices of altcoins are likely to follow even if there are positive news about them.

Similarly, when the price of Bitcoin rises significantly over a short time period, it would signal that a huge sum of money is entering the market. Prices of altcoins may experience a slight drop as traders capitalise on the upwards BTC price actions but will eventually rise again as the money trickles into the altcoins. As the saying goes, a rising tide raises all boats.

As such, what we want to look out for is this sharp rise or drop in Bitcoin's price. The usual day-to-day buy and sell orders can have between 5% to 20% of fluctuation. If there is a significant piece of news, there will be a sustained rise or drop day over day, which means a compounded effect of 20% to 50% in a week. This pattern is typical of strong bullish or bearish market sentiments.

However, when whales enter or exit the market, the impact is a price fluctuation between 20% to 50% within a single day. This does not happen all the time and is usually observed after a prolonged period of bullish or bearish activity when prices seem to be nearing an all-time high or low.

When buying cryptocurrencies, we want to look for the upwards trend in the market. Simply by following the price action of Bitcoin, we can make our best guess as to whether the movement is due to normal market sentiments or the influx of money from institutions and whales. Both instances present good profiting opportunities but the big movement triggered by whales will be easier to catch without any technical knowledge.

iii. Find the inflection points

Keeping in mind that the entries and exits of institutions and whales can cause dramatic fluctuations in prices, we can use this knowledge to identify the points of inflection.

Inflection points are critical price levels where the market reverses and makes a sudden surge or drop after stagnating for a while. The common pattern is that the surge or dip has a magnitude of over 20% within an hour. The reason is that there is an extremely large buy or sell order that moves the prices.

What happens after the surge is that the rest of the market will help to perpetuate the momentum of the price movement, which is quickly followed by a slight market correction. Hence, an upwards price movement will continue for a short while before dropping back slightly.

We can capitalise on the inflection points by observing the price patterns of Bitcoin or Ethereum, and follow as closely as possible to the inflection points. This will net you a quick 10–20% profit in a couple of days when the market moves upwards. Alternatively, you can use support and resistance levels to find the likely zones where these inflection points will occur.

As this is a short-term trade, it is extremely important to take profits when the market is on the rise. The market will most likely correct and you will be back to square one, which means that you would have wasted time and energy and you might have performed just as well or better if you had just bought and held for the long-term.

Understanding Market Psychology

Besides the big players, retail investors are a key demographic in the cryptocurrency market. Cryptocurrency is accessible to anyone and a large majority of the market are your typical non-savvy, follow-the-crowd, buy-the-rumour-sell-the-news type of investors. As trading in the market is a zero-sum game, these are the people whom you will make your profits off. Thus, it is useful to learn about the psychology of human behaviour and how the typical person would respond to market changes.

i. Recognise herding behaviour

In a group setting, when an individual first joins the group, he looks at the actions of others in the group to determine how he should behave. This is the concept of social influence and conformity. In the absence of explicitly stated rules, people who are new to a group reference their behaviour by modelling the rest of the group.

Similarly, when an investor enters the cryptocurrency market for the first time and there are no indicative ways for him to respond or behave, he will likely look at others to find his own bearings. This could be reading up on cryptocurrency publications, public technical analyses, or simply following the price trends in the market. This is how most investors lose in cryptocurrencies.

You should have gotten the sense of how the whales are manipulating the market while the rest of the market reacts by following. Having a large number of uninformed investors is in fact the blind leading the blind, which is what constitutes the herding behaviour in the cryptocurrency market.

Pump-and-dump groups utilise this effect to make money off the blind followers. These unorthodox groups orchestrate massive buy-ins of cryptocurrencies with low trading volume. When existing buy orders for that particular chosen coin are filled, the new inflated buy orders initiated by the pump-and-dump group kicks in and prices soar.

The surging prices create a sense of urgency for the rest of the market to blindly jump in, and when prices are all pumped up, the initial group then dump their holdings for profits. Prices plummet back to prior levels and the blind speculators who bought at the high are left stranded with a bunch of coins in losing positions.

The effects of FOMO (Fear of Missing Out) and FUD (Fear, Uncertainty, Doubt) are what drive the uninformed investor to follow blindly.

> ### What is FUD?
>
> Fear, uncertainty, and doubt (FUD) was a term that arose in the early days of the computers and was used as a PR (public relations) technique to influence the less-than-knowledgeable market on the developments of computer and software. By fabricating negative news, they create anxiety and panic in the market, so as to cause a market sell-off. When prices fall, that is when the fear mongers buy the dip and enter the market.
>
> The term gained popularity again with the rise of Bitcoin, describing how the more technical people or PR people sought to drive fear and panic amongst the average investor. Today, it is commonly used to describe groundless news and rumours, whose sole aim is to cause anxiety in the cryptocurrency market that will lead to a sell-off of coins and the dipping of prices.

ii. Know the proportion of holders (or HODLers)

The price of a cryptocurrency is determined by the market demand. As long as the buyer's desired price matches that of the seller, a transaction will occur. When buying sentiments are greater than selling sentiments, prices go up, and vice versa.

On another hand, there are a group of people called HODLers. These are people who adopt a long-term buy-and-hold strategy and are unlikely to trigger buy or sell orders just because of short-term price volatility. Their objective is to make bigger profits and they will eventually sell when prices are high enough.

There are also the HODLers who bought at the highs and are in losing positions. These people will become sellers when prices of the cryptocurrencies go back to the price levels that they bought at and they will sell near the break-even price.

HODLers choke up a portion of the circulating supply and the more HODLers there are, the smaller the actual circulating supply. In a bullish market, having more HODLers mean that prices are more likely to rise exponentially. In a bearish market, the presence and unwavering support of HODLers keep the market afloat even after a 70-80% decline in prices. Hence, HODLers are very important players in the cryptocurrency market.

> ### What is HODL?
>
> HODL (Hold on for dear life) arose in the age of the Internet talks. It came about as a typing error for "hold" when someone on the forum was appealing for others to hold on to their cryptocurrencies instead of selling them.
>
> The Internet lingo caught on and gained a form of its own, and someone else coined an acronym for it. Whether it means "hold on for dear life" or "hold", the idea is simply to just keep possession of your coins at all cost.

A cryptocurrency advocate or a long-term investor should aim to be a HODLer. However, to be profitable on your investment, you have to transit to become a seller. As such, be disciplined when your price targets are met and do not fall in love with your coins. They are just tools to help you grow your money.

Lastly, if you were to consider the proportion of HODLers in a cryptocurrency's ecosystem, you might be able to guess the likelihood of it surviving in the long run. Some cryptocurrencies have transparently laid out wallet balances online. Although it does not track how many wallets an individual owns, keeping track of the total number of wallets and the proportion of the balance can be a meaningful statistic.

iii. Tendency for loss aversion

Warren Buffett is commonly quoted for his saying that you should "be fearful when others are greedy and be greedy when others are fearful". The idea of that is to go against conventional crowd wisdom and to overcome the emotions of fear and greed.

In psychology, the loss aversion theory tells us that people have a preference to avoid losses than to make gains of a similar amount. That is to say, people would rather not lose $10 than to gain $10. The tendency to perceive the loss frame more strongly is what keeps people from putting down their money.

In cryptocurrency, the potential returns in the hundreds and thousands of percent may be enticing but the loss frame of losing all that money is stronger. Furthermore, there are many different risk factors and histories of hacks and scams that exemplify this loss frame. It is thus understandable that most people today would choose to stay away from cryptocurrencies.

Whether it is the risk of non-adoption, regulatory risks, threats of hacks and scams, or the risk of sending your coins to a wrong address, these uncertainties will always be there for as long as cryptocurrencies are not mainstream. We should not take risks blindly but we should be aware that we humans have a tendency to avoid losses.

Investments are about weighing the potential gains against the risk and about risk management, so we cannot focus solely on the loss frames and avoid investing altogether.

Chapter Summary

The cryptocurrency market is accessible to everyone from market manipulators to mom-and-pop investors. The combination of investors coming from all walks of life can have profound effects on the market. It also makes it an exciting playground for trading and investing.

Cryptocurrency trading is a zero-sum game and people grow their wealth at the expense of the people who follow the market blindly and make losses. You can complain about the unfairness of the market and about life but it probably will not change anything. Instead, you can use this knowledge to your advantage and make profits from the uprise of cryptocurrencies.

The most important takeaway from this chapter is to look at the market from another perspective – one that is not based on fundamentals or technicals.

Take a step back and utilise a second level of thinking so as to anticipate the market movements and capitalise on it. It could be riding along the trend or going against the norm. Be aware of the market forces and your own psychological inclinations so that you can play the market and not be played by it.

III: Through The Looking Glass – The Future Beholds

Alice laughed. "There's no use trying," she said, "One can't believe impossible things."

"I daresay you haven't had much practice," said the Queen. "When I was your age, I always did it for half-an-hour a day. Why, sometimes I believed as many as six impossible things before breakfast."

Chapter 7
Common Arguments Against Cryptocurrencies
What are the risks and assumptions when investing in cryptoassets?

Cryptocurrencies can generate huge return on investments because it is relatively new to the masses and there are no proper valuation methods yet. Speculation is rife as people guesstimate how much cryptoassets are worth while grappling with the constantly evolving regulations. This volatile and speculative environment attracts the most seasoned of Wall Street traders and young, savvy investors.

Whilst there may be plenty of potential upsides, it is important to reflect on the threats and be critical of the assumptions that we make regarding decentralisation and cryptocurrencies. I believe that any forms of change will be met with resistance and we have to be wary of these barriers.

Whether it is individuals or institutions who are against this ideological change, the technology has to stand against the criticisms and prove itself in the long run. Only then, will we have a truly decentralised economy.

The Promise of Decentralisation

Bitcoin is the first ever cryptocurrency, and it was the pipe dream of programmers and cryptographers. Its origins can be traced back to a group of cypherpunks. 'Cipher' refers to the secret-message-and-cryptography aspect of the technology while 'punks' describes the type of people who deviate from social norms. This group of cypherpunks had experimented with variations of digital currency for a while, but it was one of them, Satoshi Nakamoto, who started Bitcoin.[18]

The first ever purchase made via Bitcoin was two pizzas that cost 10,000 BTC. Today, that would amount to millions of dollars but it was never about the money. That transaction was monumental as it was proof that an alternative monetary system could work.

As more people gradually learnt about and understood Bitcoin, more and more coin exchanges emerged and Bitcoin became even more accessible to a normal person. Several e-commerce sites and restaurants also started to offer Bitcoin as a payment option.

Interestingly, Bitcoin was not the first instance of a digital currency. Around the millennium, the Internet proliferated with tangible use cases like cloud computing and e-commerce. One US company, Gold & Silver Reserve Inc, came up with the concept of the trading of digital gold via a website. The website was a channel to buy and sell gold, which they held physical quantities of in a safety deposit box.

The company amassed millions of users and even implemented its own API (application programming interface), which means that other applications and website can connect to e-gold and tap on it as a payment solution. At its peak, e-gold was accepted by multiple websites and some even offered the trading of e-gold with fiat currencies, which is much like a currency exchange.

---

[18] To this day, the identity of Satoshi Nakamoto remains unknown. Hal Finney, who was one of the contributors to Bitcoin, received Bitcoins directly from Nakamoto himself on the day of its release.

E-gold was also divisible into smaller units and was one of the first online micropayment using an asset. The company became very successful not just for normal monetary transfers but also for facilitating criminal activities and money laundering. Eventually, e-gold's business was shut down by the government as they did not have proper KYC procedures in place to prevent criminal activities and they did not manage to obtain the required money transmitting licenses.

Nonetheless, e-gold proved a concept and showed that there was demand for a digital monetary service. One of the biggest weaknesses of e-gold was that it was centralised. Centralising a digital store of value puts it at risk of being attacked by malicious actors or shut down by the authorities, which was the eventual demise of e-gold when the company had to adhere to the cease-and-desist orders from the government.

Similarly, the subprime mortgage crisis was a problem of centralisation. It was an oversight by financial institutions who oversold mortgage-backed securities (MBS) and related mortgage-based products, which led to the eventual bank-run after the burst of the housing bubble in 2008. Despite being responsible for investors' money, these financial institutions over-leveraged and had to write off their holdings of subprime MBS eventually, causing investors who trusted them to suffer losses.

Hence, Bitcoin is an attractive alternative to money as it is not created or managed by a centralised company. The promise of decentralisation is that there will not be a single point of failure that can cripple the system. No government institutions can forcefully shut down the system as they did with e-gold, nor will Bitcoin suffer from a bank run. Furthermore, decentralisation has the potential to cut out intermediaries to enable a truly peer-to-peer economy.

Cryptocurrencies are like a democratised form of money and their price values, the frequency of transactions, the dynamics of their respective ecosystems are all dependent on their users.

Governments cannot prevent the use of it but they can implement measures to deter the use of it.

For example, they can regulate coin exchanges and institutions that offer cryptocurrency-related services and derivatives, which helps them protect their own fiat currency and prevent illegal trades and money laundering[19]. Simple monitoring of the gateways between fiat money and cryptocurrencies and strict KYC measures would suffice for now, but stricter rules and laws may be implemented in future.

The takeaway here is that decentralisation promises an alternative – a utopia, where the economy is not governed by any institutions and is instead self-running.

However, we cannot assume that decentralisation will come soon. As of now, there are limitations like limited transaction rates, high transaction fees, and complexity of usage, which make the cost of switching high. There must be significant improvements and perhaps major crises like that of 2008 to push people to make the switch towards cryptocurrencies.

When the limitations and the regulatory concerns are resolved, the decentralisation utopia will arrive, eventually.

---

[19] Silk Road was a website that facilitated anonymous transactions of drugs and firearms in Bitcoin, and was later shut down by the authorities. However, they cannot shut down Bitcoin per se.

The Uncertainty of State Regulations

Even though cryptocurrencies are decentralised, governments can still enact their power over companies offering cryptocurrency-related products and on their citizens. China, for example, was one of the first to impose extreme standards on cryptocurrency exchanges; most other countries enforce strict KYC measures instead of a blanket ban of fiat-to-cryptocurrency exchanges. China has also put a ban on mining operations in the country.

Although there are many arguments against cryptocurrencies, citing illegal activities and the funding of terrorist activities, most governments are still keeping an open stance to cryptocurrencies. This is not only to embrace innovation but it also allows them to tax their citizens for their gains from trading or mining of cryptocurrencies. Cryptocurrency taxes are known to be as high as 55% in Japan while some other countries still do not impose any taxes on cryptocurrency gains.

As cryptocurrencies are still relatively unstable and risky, it might actually be better that cryptocurrencies remain relatively inaccessible until the general public is properly educated on how to use it safely. That is why it makes sense for regulations to slowly develop so that it does not generate overly positive news that would lead to an overly bullish market outlook and citizens taking on mortgages to dabble in cryptocurrencies.

The regulatory space is definitely on most people's watch list as any major support or bans can have a rippling effect globally. Whether cryptocurrencies will be illegal to use, whether there will be taxes on cryptocurrency gains, and whether cryptocurrencies will be worth anything, governments' acceptance of cryptocurrencies can influence their eventual state of adoption. Indeed, these factors are legitimate concerns and are investment risks but I feel that regulations should be taken positively as they allow the cryptocurrency space to mature safely and steadily.

The Possibility of a Speculative Bubble

One major criticism of cryptocurrency is that prices are soaring too quickly. Its growth is unsustainable and will eventually burst, like a bubble. Firstly, we should understand what constitutes a bubble.

> *The first ever financial bubble*
>
> One interesting piece of history that people like to compare Bitcoin with is Tulip Mania. In the 1930s, there was a hysteric and hyped up demand for the Dutch tulips. Tulips and its bulbs became so valuable, the most expensive and rarest of them were known to be traded for houses.
>
> Tulips were beautiful. They were scarce, seasonal, and hard to cultivate. It was also the time where the rich aristocrats would spend a fortune on art, and so speculating on tulips was not inconceivable.
>
> While demand was high, what caused the bubble to grow was in part supply and demand, and in part the futures contract. When the tulips were in still in cultivation, the farmers agreed on a price to sell the entire batch of tulips. This became the first form of a futures contract. The owner of the contract has the right to purchase the batch of tulips at the price. These contracts can be later sold and contracts were known to be traded across multiple hands in a day.
>
> The bubble burst and Tulip Mania came to an end due to a variety of reasons, including sellers making enough and exiting the market and the fear that arose because most of the traded bulbs were not even in existence. The sudden and heavy sell-off of the future contracts led to the sharp decline of tulip prices and the bubble's burst[17].

A financial bubble describes the price of an investment that rises so sharply beyond its intrinsic value such that when people discover the true value, which is significantly lower, it triggers a massive sell-off that causes prices to plummet. The bubble has thus popped with prices falling as sharply as it has risen. Bubbles grow as a result of people's unrealistic expectations and overly hyped up valuations.

If we were to look at the modern history of bubbles there are a few notable examples. The subprime mortgage crisis came about when the property market was bullish and prices of property seemed like it would never drop again. Loans were issued with low interest rates and to less than ideal borrowers. However, when the stock market started to rise while the demand for housing went down and the interest rate went up, prices of the properties fell. The subprime borrowers who were not able to service their loans defaulted on payment as the loans that they had to pay were more expensive than the value of their properties that were bought at a high. The rapidly declining housing prices was thus the burst of the housing bubble.

The Dotcom bubble is similar to cryptocurrency in many areas as it was driven by the promise of a new technology and its hype. People caught on to the trend and had a '.com' in everything they created just as they would 'blockchain' everything today and valuations will rise magically. VC funding was rampant and almost groundless in the Dotcom period just like how ICOs today are raising funds with just a conceptual White Paper.

When the market eventually realised the true valuations of most of these technology and Internet companies, prices came crashing down. Many of these companies closed. Nonetheless, the aftermath of the bubble was the emergence of technology giants who had proper businesses and did real work in utilising and advancing the Internet. These are the likes of Amazon and e-commerce stores and was later followed by the social media platforms.

The cryptocurrency bubble is a call for concern as it has an extremely high trajectory of prices and no means of proper market valuation. However, if you were to liken it to the Dotcom bubble, we should be thinking of the value created by cryptocurrencies and pick the ones with strong fundamentals that will survive in the long run.

Cryptocurrencies: A non-conforming bubble?

What is the value of cryptocurrency? Indeed, for an alpha stage or beta stage product, current price valuations may be too high. However, the contrary may also be true. If Bitcoin and cryptocurrencies were to work better than existing systems, could it be plausible that current prices are undervalued?

The cryptocurrency market exhibits a bubble-like chart and the bubble has already burst multiple times. Each time it burst, the market recovers and pushes beyond its previous highs. In the course of history, burst bubbles do not grow again. Does this mean that it is not a bubble or are we in a different kind of bubble? What causes the bubble to inflate?

Diagram 9. BTC price floor adjustments. Screenshot from coinmarketcap.com.

In cryptocurrency, each time the market 'bursts', it is the result of the majority of the people selling off due to poor market sentiments. These people could be knowledgeable investors who are timing the market to take profits and enter again at the dips. It could also be speculators who realise the overvaluation and want to cut their losses. The interesting phenomenon is that the market grows again, possibly because there are new entrants to the market who suddenly realise the "undervaluation" of prices.

The bottomed out prices at the end of each 'burst' bubble is like a price floor that indicates the low end of market valuation, which could be the true valuation of cryptocurrencies. With each 'burst' bubble, the price floor is gradually adjusted and the market appears to be closer to an accurate valuation.

The sharp rises and declines on the price chart of Bitcoin are the bubble-like patterns and are the speculative aspect of the market. If we were to ignore these spikes, the price floor is generally on a steady upward climb over the past decade (gradual sloping blue arrow in Diagram 9). Can this growth be sustained forever?

I believe so, and that it will continue to grow perpetually just like technology, population, life expectancy, and living standards. There will be normal levels of attrition but it will not stop growing unless we hit an Ice Age or if Thanos snaps his fingers[20].

One thing is for sure. The burgeoning-and-bursting price cycles show that most participants in the market do not know yet if the asset is truly over or undervalued. It also hints at a likelihood of market manipulation by the people with money and who knows the potential of cryptocurrencies.

New entrants to the market are all speculating on the true value of cryptocurrencies. Institutions may not be that knowledgeable either and may just be diversifying their bets.

Instead of staying out of the market and telling others that we are in a bubble, which is apparent, how can we make use of the bubble cycles to our advantage and profit from it? If the market is being manipulated, how can we profit from this manipulation by riding alongside the market manipulators?

---

[20] Life expectancy and living standards has been growing at an alarming rate. Our resources are depleting faster than they are replenished. The reference to Ice Age or Thanos describes the scenario where the population is wiped out, and in Thanos' view, it resets to a sustainable level where the remaining half of the population can flourish in.

As it stands today, cryptoassets have the potential to become the next stock market or derivatives market where people trade and speculate on a daily basis. For now, it will not displace those markets as it is way too volatile and still a work in progress. Perhaps, it is inevitable that cryptocurrency has to exhibit bubble-like characteristics in order to gain attention and to foster mainstream adoption.

The Sustainability of Mining

The concept of mining comes from the natural mining of minerals where miners excavate the resources from the ground. These workers traded their effort to extract precious metals like gold, which will be later traded on the market.

For Bitcoin, there will be a total of 21 million units. Mining comes down to the work that miners do, which is validating transactions on the new block and adding the new block to the chain. Thereafter, miners are rewarded for their work in coins and are paid Bitcoins for their block reward. That is to say, they are rewarded based on their "proof-of-work".

The argument against the mining of cryptocurrencies is that it consumes a large amount of energy just to validate transactions. Regardless of the source of the energy needed to drive the computers, mining uses energy and deprives the world of it. Hence, many people question the sustainability of mining. What many of them overlook is that mining is just one way of achieving consensus in a distributed ledger.

i. Proof-of-Work (POW): Effort-based reward system

The work that miners do is to validate the transactions in a new block so that it can be added to the previous block, therein extending the chain of transactions. To add the new block, they have to use their computers and a lot of electricity, to cryptographically decrypt and inscribe the transactions onto the digital ledger.

However, only one miner who successfully adds the new block gets the reward. The miner who adds the block submits his proof-of-work and the new block online so that other miners can update their ledgers and continue to validate the next block. All these competition amongst miners is for the block reward, which means that there may be excessive resources consumed just to validate one block of transactions.

The block reward for Bitcoin started out to be worth 50 BTC and after every interval, the reward is halved. The block reward was reduced to 25 BTC on November 28, 2012, was further reduced to 12.5 BTC on July 9, 2016, and will be halved all the way until all 21 Million units of BTC have been issued.

> ## How do you mine Bitcoins?
>
> When you set up your computer to mine Bitcoins, you are trying to solve a complex cryptographic equation that can only be solved by plugging in random answers (or hashes). The faster your computer, the more hashes you can input per second, and the likelihood of resolving that block increases.
>
> Today, most mining is done using graphics cards or ASIC miners. Graphics cards or GPU (Graphic Processing Unit) were originally designed for high-performance gaming and software usage but are also effective for mining. ASIC (Application-Specific Integrated Circuit) are computers designed solely for mining and cannot be used for any other purpose. What ASIC lacks in functionality is made up for by its relatively low cost and high efficiency for mining. However, if mining becomes obsolete, so will ASIC miners.

When all 21M Bitcoins are issued, the incentive for miners to continue to validate transactions will come from a fraction of the total transacted sum in the block. That is to say, miners will not get newly minted coins but are instead rewarded with the transaction fees in Bitcoin. There is an underlying assumption that miners will continue to service the transactions because the transaction fees will be worth something. Miners will also most likely to have broken even on their hardware costs so their cost of mining will only be the electricity bills. Hence, this scenario assumes that the cost of mining will remain low relative to the transaction fees because Bitcoin will have been widely adopted by then and transactions are frequent.

As prices of Bitcoin continue to rise, the block rewards become more attractive and more people will jump onboard mining. As competition increases, it becomes even harder to successfully mine the new block so miners begin to pool their computing power to be the first to add the new blocks, thereby coalescing into mining pools. A mining pool, which has significantly more computing power than an individual computer is more likely to be successful in adding the next block. After which, the mining pool splits up the block reward proportionately to the miners' contribution of work. Today, it is almost impossible to mine a new block of Bitcoin solely by using your personal computer.

Conversely, if competition is too intense or if the price of Bitcoin drops, it becomes less attractive to mine so there will be an attrition of miners. If the market picks up again, then more miners will surface again. The idea is for the economics of supply and demand to play out by itself.

If POW mining indeed consumes too much unnecessary energy, then there are alternative methods of validating transactions which may be the future of cryptocurrencies. As you will see later, there are also limitations to these systems.

ii. Proof-of-stake (POS): A more energy-efficient system?

Instead of using a lot of computers and electricity to cryptographically add the next block, some people are suggesting that we use a less energy consuming method to validate transactions. In POS, the total supply of coins does not change; no block rewards are issued. Instead, the workers (now called forgers instead of miners) are rewarded the transaction fees incurred by the transactions within the block.

In a POS system, forgers have to stake a portion of their own coins to validate the new block. Upon successful validation, the new block will be added cryptographically to the chain, and the forgers who participated will be rewarded a number of coins proportionate to their stake. This reward concept is similar to being paid transaction fees but you show your proof-of-stake rather than your proof-of-work.

Staking reduces the cryptographic difficulty. The more coins staked to the block, the greater the reduction in transaction difficulty of the cryptogram, and the more likely for the block of transactions to be validated and added. Hence, the blockchain is still linked cryptographically but what has changed is a staking system instead of a mining system.

The more coins staked, the faster the block will be resolved. The more coins a forger stakes, the greater his proportion of the reward. However, a new issue arises as people who have more coins can afford to stake more and get paid more, which means that the rich get richer.

Several solutions are being tested to reduce the likelihood of this scenario. For example, it could be limiting a maximum number of coins that one can stake or to randomly select a different group of forgers each round. The Delegate POS (DPOS[21]) system is an adaptation of POS such that a number of delegates are elected based on their holding supply, their transaction activity, amongst other factors to participate in each staking round. Each round of validation may involve a new set of delegates, and bad actors will be prevented from future rounds.

While POS theoretically uses less electricity and computing power, there are existing limitations to the system that are still being resolved. How can we ensure a sustainable and fair reward system? How can bad actors be punished? What we have to keep in mind is that these are just ways to achieve consensus because of the distributed ledger. The value of DLT lies in its merits of distribution and decentralisation.

---

[21] In ARK's DPOS system, anyone who wants to be a delegate have to write a proposal that describes his contribution to the ecosystem and the community (anyone who owns ARK) can respond with their votes. Only the Top 51 voted-in delegates can participate in the forging and these delegates may be replaced when they lose votes.

The Threat of Security Lapses

As cryptocurrency is somewhat in its beta stage, it is vulnerable to security lapses. This includes programming shortcomings, users using the system wrongly, and hackers stealing from or attacking the system.

i. System vulnerabilities and limitations

One of the much talked about issues is a DDOS attack where hackers attempt to disrupt the service. In Bitcoin and similar POW-typed cryptocurrencies, a DDOS attack would mean that the attackers have more than 51% of the mining power such that they can create a falsified chain and have the majority of the mining power to acknowledge this incorrect blockchain as the main chain, thus disrupting the newer blocks of transactions.

There have been past incidents where mining pools managed to accumulate close to half the total mining power[22]. However, Bitcoin mining pools themselves recognise that this scenario is detrimental for the blockchain and have pledged to cap their mining power at a lower threshold.

Other coins like Verge (XVG) were not as fortunate, which was hit by two incidents of DDOS attacks and over US$1M in funds were stolen in April and May 2018.

Besides external attacks, the infancy of the programming languages may also be a shortcoming of cryptocurrencies. In November 2017, due to a loophole in the programming language for Ethereum (Solidity), a novice programmer triggered a malfunctioning code which froze the funds of addresses in some wallets. The affected users were using a programme by Parity, and the incident was thus labelled the "Parity wallet freeze".

---

[22] The bigger the proportion of mining power accumulated, the more probable a DDOS attack; a DDOS-double-spending attempt can happen at 40% and is increasingly probable as the fraction increases.

Although the Parity incident was not a malicious attack, it reminded the rest of us that cryptocurrencies are still a work in progress and are still subjected to such vulnerabilities. The Parity incident awaits to be resolved and affected users have their funds stranded for the time being[23].

Another way for a user to lose his funds is if he sends the funds to a non-account because of a typing error. There is no way to reverse the transaction as this is the immutable quality of blockchain technology, so the funds will be lost forever. If users forget where they store the coins or their account passwords and their seed backups, their funds will also be lost forever. That is why it is very important to have multiple copies of your seed and private keys stored securely across different channels.

It will take some time and perhaps more incidents for cryptocurrencies to mature and become usable for the average person. It will also take more education for that person to use and transact cryptocurrencies safely and securely.

ii. Users fallibility

The inadequacy of users has also led to many other examples of lost funds. Early in 2018, many owners of IOTA discovered that coins were being withdrawn from their wallets. The reason for the 'hack' was because these users had created their seed addresses on an online generator.

As it is troublesome to generate your own seed address in IOTA, many people resorted to an online generator, which turned out to have recorded and stored these addresses. Seed addresses in IOTA are akin to your private keys and the hackers of the seed generator later accessed the users' wallets and withdrew their funds.

Another way that hackers can steal your funds is by attacking your computer. It could be planting a malware (malicious software)

---

[23] Some of the affected users are organisations and businesses, and have proposed to "unfreeze" the funds in the next hard fork. However, their solutions have not been accepted by the majority.

with your online downloads, which is usually a keylogger that tracks whatever you type and enter. The keylogger then sends these information to the hacker.

It could also be hackers snooping users on a public wi-fi or creating malicious hotspots for unsuspecting users to tap on. Snooping is the use of a software to read any packets of information you try to send via the Internet connection, so the log-in details and other confidential information entered will be snooped by these hackers.

Phishing scams and cyber attacks like these have been around since the days of the Internet. It is not unique to cryptocurrencies. Hence, if you are using your computer to access precious funds, be very wary about the downloading of unsafe software especially from unknown developers. When you are in public, do refrain from using public wi-fi or the hotspots of unknown users because you are compromising your accounts. Lastly, be wary of using online generators and websites asking you for your private keys.

iii. Hacks on coin exchanges

Given the sky-high value of Bitcoin and other cryptocurrencies, there have been numerous attempts of theft on coin exchanges. Coin exchanges are a prime target because they hold the funds of all their customers. **The lesson here is: Move your coins from the exchange's wallet into your own private wallet.**

Mt Gox (2014)

The Mt Gox incident remains one of the biggest hacks to date with about 850,000 BTCs worth around US$400,000 then stolen from Mt Gox, one of the biggest coin exchanges at that point in time. The hackers had stolen the funds over a period of two years but Mt Gox was still operating and servicing BTC trades despite missing up to 80,000 BTCs since 2011.

The stolen BTCs had been transferred and laundered so the sum of coins cannot be traced any further. Mt Gox was bankrupted as it could not refund its users in lost funds. However, about 200,000 remaining BTC were found in a Mt Gox archive, which had an estimated value of over US$4B when BTC prices soared to US$20,000 in December 2017. The once bankrupted Mt Gox had somehow become solvent because the price of its remaining assets appreciated in value. This was an unprecedented event.

A trustee was appointed to sell the funds and return victims the dollar value equivalent in losses rather than a proportionate amount in BTC. Had the victims received BTC instead, they would be sitting at over 1000% gains from when the coins were stolen from them.

Coincheck (2018)

You might think that coin exchanges would learn from the lessons of others and step up on their security measures but lapses still occur. Early in 2018, 500 million NEM coins were stolen from Japanese exchange Coincheck with a value of over US$500,000 at the point of the hack.

In this case, the stolen funds were immediately traced to the hacker's accounts and tagged as stolen funds to warn other exchanges from transacting with these accounts. Coincheck also promised to return victims their stolen funds.

Binance (2018)

Binance is one of the biggest cryptocurrency-to-cryptocurrency exchanges in the world and was targeted by a group of hackers in March 2018. This time, hackers targeted users on the exchange rather than the exchange's wallet itself and their attempt was foiled by Binance.

Users who were affected used a trading bot that automated buy and sell trades. The creators of the trading bots added a 'backdoor', which gave them access to the users' accounts. The hackers made use of the low trading volume of Viacoins (VIA) and put up expensive sell orders on their own accounts.

When they have accumulated a decent number of user accounts and funds, they logged on to these accounts and bought up all the overpriced VIA from their accounts, so the BTC of the hacked accounts went into the hackers' accounts.

Fortunately, Binance had a security function that halted transactions if there was a sudden and unusual surge in trading patterns. The hackers' attempt was halted within two minutes and the manipulated trades reversed. The trades of legitimate VIA sell orders had to be executed so a very small portion of users was affected.

The Binance incident turned out to be a positive example as the coin exchange had stringent security measures in place and was thus able to prevent malicious attempts by hackers. However, for your funds to be truly safe, you should always move them to your own private wallet.

After all, cryptocurrency exchanges are centralised institutions, so if you buy into the idea of decentralisation, you really should take your cryptocurrencies off the coin exchanges.

There are security risks today that are still being worked out just like the many other limitations of DLT. It is because of these downsides that cryptocurrencies today come at a bargain. If we take the effort to learn and take adequate measures to protect ourselves, we can reduce our risk of investments and the eventual reward can be a significant bonus.

The Speculation Fuelled by The Media

The news and rumours framed by the media can influence the cryptocurrency market greatly. Today, the media is not solely represented by mainstream news channels but also encompasses a wide range of social influencers, authoritative cryptocurrency-related publications, and even independent traders and bloggers. Most newcomers to cryptocurrencies assume that the media is objective and even if they are not, the diversified viewpoints would provide a balanced argument.

However, with such a wide variety of opinions, there is often a misrepresentation of cryptocurrencies and a lack of objectivity in the media reports. As implied by the agenda setting theory, the media shapes the way that people think. The short-term impact of these rumours and news are speculative price changes but the long-term consequence is that it shapes the way and the rate of cryptocurrency adoption.

For example, it could be triggering negative or biased sentiments so as to influence regulatory frameworks. It could also be an intentional attempt by Internet giants like Facebook and Google to restrict the type of news on the Internet[24]. Another way would be the imposition of media silence on cryptocurrency-related topics on mainstream media.

For cryptocurrencies to reach mainstream adoption, people have to be informed and educated and the media plays an important role in all of these. Although we have little say and control over what the media presents, we should be aware of their biases and refrain from taking a stance that is based solely on what the media tells us. We should also be aware that the media can influence cryptocurrency prices in the short run, which is something that short-term traders have to pay attention to.

---

[24] Facebook and Google have officially banned cryptocurrency-related advertisements for prolonged periods. However, even if it is unofficial, it is conceivable that the results we find on Google are already filtered.

Chapter Summary

There are many threats and assumptions surrounding the cryptocurrency space, which are all risk factors in our consideration of cryptocurrencies as an investment. These factors can influence the rate of cryptocurrency and DLT adoption.

I try to look at these threats as double-edged swords.

Regulations can shut off innovation but they are necessary for cryptocurrencies to be adopted and used safely. Security lapses can affect and deter users but these are lessons that improve our overall understanding and knowledge of the cryptocurrency space. The bubble-like characteristic of cryptocurrency prices is questionable but it appears to be an inevitable step for the space to mature.

The early days of the wild wild west are often fraught with uncertainties and dangers. However, these are what presents us with the opportunity to buy cryptocurrencies at a bargain. As an investor, it is important to be aware of these risks but it is equally important to learn and understand the technology as this knowledge reduces your risk of investment.

What we have to consider then is the basis for these threats and whether they will be resolved in the long run. I believe that with increased dissemination of the right information, new methods of consensus, and a nurturing regulatory framework, these kinks will iron out.

Perhaps then, it is only a matter of when cryptocurrencies will become mainstream.

Chapter 8
Looking Beyond Today's Noise And Speculation
How can we deal with the volatile market and look towards an alternate future?

Cryptocurrency is multidisciplinary and there are no restrictions to where you start. The technology enthusiasts may be drawn by blockchain programming or hardware mining while people in the finance industry may be concerned about how their industries will be disrupted by blockchain technology.

For most people, the draw of cryptocurrencies is likely the chance for them to grow their money after witnessing the exponential growth of cryptocurrency prices during a bull run. Regardless of your motivation, there will be a lot to pick up and this book serves to be that handy guidebook, which caters especially to the last group of people.

Some of you might have heard of people drawing parallels between cryptocurrency and "going down the rabbit hole". Just like Alice's adventure in Wonderland, which is whimsical, bizarre, and full of uncertainties, your crypto journey will likely start off in a somewhat nonsensical fashion.

Down this rabbit hole, first-time investors will most definitely be overwhelmed with surprises, question marks, and emotional outbursts. The soaring coin prices can bring about excitement, disbelief, and suspense while the down cycles of the market can leave one disappointed and even despondent.

Just when you think that you have mastered the market cycle or certain topics, when you think that you have gotten your bearings, the next wave hits you and displaces you into a completely new environment. Would you be at a tea party next or will you be beheaded by The Queen[25]?

When we are thrown into an unfamiliar environment, we use our senses and existing knowledge to try to make sense of the unknown. That is why people try to use existing benchmarks to evaluate and make sense of cryptocurrencies but these measures often fall short or have their limitations.

Down this rabbit hole, whether you are overwhelmed by the extensive technical knowledge or by the ruthless and unpredictable market, the goal of this chapter is to remind you that you are not alone in the journey; many others have encountered and faced a similar experience.

If you ever feel powerless against the market, you should take a breather from investing and trading to explore the technical side of things. You might make mistakes and the market may not work in your favour but what is more important is that you learn and you come back stronger.

By learning, you will start to appreciate decentralisation, and you will be aware of the advantages and the caveats of cryptocurrencies. By learning, you are taking that first step through the looking glass and into the utopia of DLT.

---

[25] In Alice's adventure, she constantly ran into unexpected events, which includes chancing upon Mad Hatter's tea party, and infuriating The Queen who then demanded for her to be beheaded.

Similarly, investing and trading cryptocurrencies can lead to all types of unexpected outcomes.

Regulating Your Emotions

The sheer amount of information and complexity of the topic on distributed ledgers can deter newcomers. However, once you get past a certain threshold and are used to most technical jargons, you will find that there is so much you can learn. For first-timers, this will be a point when you are constantly aroused by the latest news in the market or fixated on the fluctuations in your portfolio.

Having gone past that phase, my advice is to slow it down. The media reports and the market changes may be fast and furious but the reality is that most development and implementations of DLT take time. Be it software development, regulatory proposals, or user adoption, they will all take a while to materialise. If you are feeling impatient, you are probably under the spell of the media because the only thing that moves and changes rapidly in the crypto space are the news reports and chatroom rumours.

Recognise what these news and rumours are selling you. Does it encourage you to buy into the hype or make you feel like you should sell off all your holdings immediately? You may feel compelled to act quickly and decisively in the cryptocurrency market but that is usually reserved for experienced traders. Remember that investing is a longer term game and you should not pay too much attention to short-term factors.

Take your time to learn the craft of trading and to experiment with different trading and investing strategies. Cryptocurrencies will not be immediately adopted, nor will they stop growing, so learn it well and prepare yourself for the decentralised future.

Lastly, remember that when you are feeling a sense of FOMO or FUD, ask yourself why you are feeling that way. Slow things down, and then, evaluate your next course of action. Play the market and try not to be played by it.

Looking At Alternative Investments

Cryptocurrency is generally more volatile and unpredictable compared to traditional investments. Market cycles are shorter and faster with 24/7 trading activity and it is relatively accessible for any type of investors.

As a general rule of investment, you should not put all your eggs in one basket, and cryptocurrency should not be the only instrument in your entire investment portfolio. I will briefly cover other investment options so that you can weigh them against cryptocurrencies and possibly diversify and invest in them.

i. Cryptocurrency VS Stock markets

Stock markets comprise of listed companies who aim to make a profit from the sale of their product or service offering. As a shareholder, you may be entitled to dividends, which is a portion of the profits generated by the company. As the company starts to generate more profit and become cash positive, investors will assign greater value to the company, which means that your share value will appreciate. As a shareholder, you also have some say in the company's decision.

The main difference between stocks and cryptocurrencies are that companies listed on the stock exchanges are centralised. They have balance sheets, profits and losses, and other metrics that allow a quantitative assessment of the "better" fundamentals. However, just like cryptocurrencies, there is also the speculative component in the price value of a stock.

Cryptocurrencies, on the other hand, do not have such benchmarks. With no ratios and numbers to quantify the price of cryptocurrencies, it is entirely speculative. Cryptocurrency companies are not aiming to generate revenue for their investors, who also have limited say in the development or implementations.

As a cryptocurrency investor, you may just be trying to make the best guess. Your faith in a cryptocurrency's potential may well be a confirmation bias where you are trying to justify your own choice of investment. As such, if you are a more conservative investor, you would probably agree with Warren Buffett's stance that "cryptocurrencies lack fundamental".

ii. Cryptocurrency VS Startups and VC funds

In recent years, startups have gotten a lot more funding and attention from angel investors, PE (private equity) firms, and VC firms. There is even the benchmark of startups that have attained the unicorn status, which is a valuation of US$1B or more. Startups typically go through multiple rounds of funding, with each successful round marking a new milestone of business and coming at higher price valuations.

In the very initial seed rounds, some startup companies have managed to raise substantial funding even though they are at the pre-product or pre-revenue stage. Investors pledge their money behind these companies for a multitude of reasons, be it the strength of the team, the size of the market, or the feasibility of the business. While startup investments are usually restricted to rich individuals who are angel investors or accredited investors, cryptocurrency investments are accessible to almost anyone today.

Investors in startup companies believe in the potential of these companies to grow so their equity stake will become more valuable in the next investment round. Likewise, buying cryptocurrencies today is believing in the token's potential to hit mainstream adoption. However, unlike startup companies, cryptocurrency investors have no say over its development. As mentioned earlier, you do not have to invest if you want to support and use a cryptocurrency. You invest only because you believe that its present value will appreciate in future.

iii. Cryptocurrency VS Foreign Exchange (FX)

Cryptocurrencies are most often compared with fiat currencies. Getting different cryptocurrencies from a coin exchange is similar to going to a money changer to change for foreign currencies. Trading these currencies is thus like playing the FX market.

While the supply of fiat money is controlled by institutions, the supply of cryptocurrencies are determined by the developers. A government can introduce different measures like increasing supply, issuing bonds, and introducing fiscal policies and trade laws to protect its currency.

The FX and cryptocurrency markets are both global markets and a piece of news in one part of the world can have a resonating impact. Many of the technical indicators can be similarly applied with slight adjustments to account for the 24/7 market and increased volatility. While people typically trade the FX market, cryptocurrencies can accommodate both short-term trades and longer term investing where you buy and store the cryptocurrencies privately.

iv. Cryptocurrency VS Other Investments

Some people liken Bitcoin to gold and Litecoin to silver. The underlying concept is the scarce supply of these cryptocurrencies. Bitcoin was programmed to have a maximum of 21 million units while Litecoin, a maximum of 84 million units.

Many people argue that this is artificial scarcity as each unit of coin can be divided infinitesimally. However, it is this illusion of scarcity alongside the merits of DLT that creates demand for these coins. That is why they assign a value to cryptocurrencies and think that it can be an alternative store of value for fiat money.

If you are looking at low-risk investments to grow your savings slowly or to hedge against inflation, stay away from cryptocurrencies. It is only worth investing if you see the potential of decentralisation or if you can allocate a portion of your portfolio to high-risk investments. In that aspect, cryptocurrency can be a speculation tool, a hedging tool, a store of value, which is the allure of this multifaceted asset.

More importantly, we should recognise how cryptocurrency is carving its own unique space as an investment vehicle — as a 'cryptoasset'.

Cutting Down On Crypto-Obsession

In the speculative cryptocurrency market, prices will take a nosedive every now and then. We are looking at dips of over 60% from all-time highs and the people who have it the hardest are investors who have entered at the higher price points. Amongst these people, there have been reported cases of anxiety, depression, and even suicides.

If you are feeling any of these symptoms during a bear market, chances are, you have invested more than you should. It is highly inadvisable to put your life savings or take on loans to enter the cryptocurrency market. Nonetheless, if you do find yourself in such a situation, take a break and stop looking at the changes in the market. You probably cannot do anything about it anyway.

For some others, it may just be a lingering soreness over a sum of money that you are prepared to lose. The down cycle presents an opportunity for you to evaluate your investment and exit strategies.

What would you have done differently and what would you do if a similar scenario arises in the future? Remember that if you are buying for the long term, short-term price fluctuations should not influence or change your strategy.

Be aware of cognitive biases like hindsight bias because it is easy to say what you should have or should not have done on hindsight. You do not have to beat yourself up over a missed opportunity. There will be plenty more in future and it always comes down to whether you seize the opportunities the next time they are presented to you.

Lastly, remember the concept of opportunity cost. The time and energy that you spend pondering over the market can be better spent with your family and friends or pursuing other hobbies. There are many other things in life besides cryptocurrencies that you can care about and devote your emotional resources on and you do not want to miss out on them.

To summarise:

1. Be conscious of your emotions. Recognise what you are feeling and identify the triggers for the anxiety, disappointment, excitement etc.

2. Look away from the prices. Recognise that the market is independent of your thoughts and actions. Be patient and let things work out by themselves.

3. Evaluate your investment strategies and plan your next course of action.

4. Be mindful of hindsight biases.

5. Spend time doing things outside of cryptocurrencies.

Distributed Ledgers: The Bridge Between Digital And Reality

Transportation technologies have changed the way we travel –from moving across land to traversing across the oceans and through the skies. Machines and industrialisation changed the system of manufacturing — there is more automation and less manual labour. The telegraph changed the system of communication while the Internet changed the way that information is stored and shared.

Over the past centuries, the common trait of these revolutionary technologies is the way they connect people. The world has become more connected than before – people are more connected physically and digitally, and consumers are more connected to businesses.

Digital connections have also become increasingly real but there is always some form of a divide between the digital world and the physical reality. For example, you cannot feel the clothes when you shop online and you cannot touch the person with whom you are talking to online.

This gap between virtual and reality cannot be perfectly reconciled, unless say teleportation happens, but it can be eased. For example, the online shopping experience can be made more realistic through a seamless experience of ordering, shipping, physically trying, and then returning of the product if it is not suitable. The divide between virtual and reality can be bridged by intermediary services who connects the physical gap.

While it makes sense to have these intermediary services to help bridge the virtual and offline world, the problem is that we might become too dependent on them. Moving forward, as this type of service becomes increasingly prevalent and pervasive in our lives, we will end up relying too much on these service providers and hence give them too much power over us. That is how Alibaba and Amazon are increasingly dominating our lives.

Enter The Digital Tokens

Blockchain and distributed ledgers changes the system of value transfer such that middlemen are cut out from the transactions; users can transact directly with one another. We have to recognise that when the tokens transfer from one person to another, any form of value can be tied to the tokens in this transaction.

Imagine this. How can I exchange one hour worth of my lawn mowing service, so that I get a lunch in return? In today's world, you have to put a price on your service, get paid in cash, which you can then spend on your lunch or on groceries. Money is the common denominator to help coordinate such daily activities, and money is a service offered by centralised institutions like the bank and the government.

However, what if through a smart contract system, you can get your remuneration for your lawn mowing service directly in the form of a lunch delivery? Or you could accumulate 10 hours of lawn mowing service to get an electric scooter as remuneration. Of course, there still must be some form of monetary value assigned so that people can measure what they are getting in return for their contributions. The core difference is that in this situation, the economic transactions do not have to be mediated by a bank.

A legal tender note assures its holder a monetary value that is recognised by the bank, so that everyone who trusts the bank can transact with one another using this monetary system. In a decentralised system, transactions between users can occur organically and be measured in tokens, as long as all participating users agree that there is value to these tokens.

The uprise of the Internet and the intermediary services have helped to bridge the gap between our digital and physical realities, but we are becoming more dependant on these intermediary services. With a layer of decentralised tokens in place, we can keep up with our demand for the physical-digital gap to be eased without depending on the centralised intermediaries.

With decentralised tokens as a common unit of accounting, people can transact with one another whether it is for money, for services, or exchange of goods just like they would use money. Furthermore, people can trust upon the code-binding smart contracts to automatically execute the transactions.

With decentralisation, societal systems can be democratised and not be regulated by a centralised organisation. Our day-to-day transactions can also happen organically between two entities, without a company to facilitate these transactions.

i. DLT and money

Remitting money from one country to another typically takes a few days or a week and through multiple intermediaries. DLT cuts down on the transaction times and cuts out the different remittance companies while lowering the transaction fees involved, greatly benefitting foreign workers around the globe.

For countries with poor fiscal policies where governments freely inflate their money freely, cryptocurrencies cut away the inefficient and corrupt centralised institutions. In countries like these[26], cryptocurrency may even be more trustable and stable than their own fiat money despite the extreme volatility today.

If centralised entities are efficient, act in the best interest of their users, and are without problems, cryptocurrency as a form of money will be less a need. That would be an idealised social capitalist system, which is unlikely to happen as there is always a need for self-preservation and self-interest. The subprime mortgage crisis and the collapse of Lehman's Brother serve as a good reminder that even mainstream big banks can be erroneous. Hence, many people consider Bitcoin and the future of decentralised money the most important revolution since the Internet.

---

[26] In countries like Zimbabwe and Venezuela, there is high demand for Bitcoin and Bitcoin's trading price in USD are in fact more expensive in these countries than in countries with more stable fiat currencies.

ii. DLT and escrows

The rise of e-commerce platforms and services like Alibaba, e-Bay, and Paypal showed that trust is a problem worth solving. Their escrow service created trust between the users and the system, and eventually trust between users. DLT promises the same service with smart contracts, with the bonus of decentralisation.

With smart contracts, peer-to-peer transactions and agreements can be made easily without having to go through some form of centralised organisation. It is still farfetched to say that you will not need lawyers, shipping companies, or any other middleman, but that is the promised state of smart contracts.

iii. DLT and societal systems

Ethereum has also enabled democratic systems with the first instance of a Decentralised Autonomous Organisation (DAO) appearing in 2016. Within a DAO, participants are issued rights in a digital format. This means that they can record, vote, and be involved, as long as they hold tokens to that DAO, which is an indication of their membership. This particular use case illustrates how governance can be mediated by a distributed ledger.

In the Ethereum DAO[27], participants pledged a portion of ETH to that organisation, which was their voting rights as to whether or not the DAO takes up a new blockchain project proposal. Similarly, a governance system can be enacted on a DAO, with tokens being issued to the citizens on a top-down basis.

The DAO would ensure equal rights in decision making or can serve as a form of monitoring and to incentivise participation within the system. Different types of economic activities can then happen on the DAO and it is an exemplar of the potential of DLT.

---

[27] The Ethereum DAO infamously led to the creation of Ethereum Classic (ETC) as it was hacked and the hackers "voted" for the funds in the DAO to be transferred to their accounts. Ethereum was forked into ETC, a version where the coins were stolen, and ETH, a new version where the funds were reversed to the state before the hack.

The Future of DLT

The blockchain is merely a way of recording values in ledgers. It is different because it is distributed and decentralised. While Bitcoin and Ethereum are considered Generation One cryptocurrencies, a new generation of cryptocurrencies have arrived. Particularly, this new generation seeks to develop and evolve the cryptocurrency space in a scalable and sustainable manner.

For example, Ethereum's Casper aims to move Ethereum away from POW mining towards POS forging, a less energy-consuming method to achieve consensus on the blockchain. ARK's Delegate POS also promises to be faster and more energy-efficient.

On another hand, IOTA utilises the Directed Acyclic Graphs (DAG) structure to achieve consensus. In IOTA, for each transaction to be validated, the device must first validate two previous transactions as a POW before that transaction can be validated by future, newer transactions. Instead of a chain-like structure, the design of IOTA's network (called Tangle) is more like a spider web that disperses outwards.

This design promises to be infinitely scalable and transactions on the network will become faster as adoption increases. IOTA is also designed to be quantum-proof as quantum computers are recognised to be a threat to blockchain mining.

Blockchain and DLT are constantly changing and improving. New applications are always being tested. It would be narrow-minded of us to merely consider cryptocurrencies for the peer-to-peer digital cash function that Bitcoin was designed to be. Cryptocurrencies can go beyond its monetary function and will potentially change all transactional processes in our daily lives.

As such, the term 'cryptocurrency' may be due for a rename as they are not just about digital currencies anymore. 'Cryptoassets', as popularised by Chris Burniske and Jack Tatar in their book *Cryptoassets: The Innovative Investor's Guide to Bitcoin and Beyond,* may be a more comprehensive term.

Today, our daily habits have already been altered and possibly restructured because of how we consume existing technologies. Our use of transportation, automated machines, smartphones, the Internet, and social media have cultivated us into a different society as what we were a decade or a century ago.

Whether we have become more efficient in our way of life or we have become more lazy and stagnant because of technology, it is all a matter of perspective.

Perhaps then, DLT merely offers a more efficient way for us to keep up with our evolved needs. Just like how social media conveniently keeps us more connected with different people, DLT is an affordance that will change transactions – more peer-to-peer transactions executed by smart contracts and without the need for an intermediary.

It may be hard to imagine the benefits of DLT when we are living in a world where centralised institutions are efficient and working. Why fix what is not broken? Hence, may I implore you to take a step through the looking glass and peek at the plausible world of decentralisation and cryptocurrencies.

Perhaps then, you might see a different reality.

Chapter Summary

As you embark on your cryptocurrency journey, you will find yourself on a rollercoaster ride. The ups and downs of the market is an experience that should be taken as a learning opportunity and a journey of self-discovery.

Regardless of whether you profit or lose money from your investments, the state of cryptocurrency will evolve and mature. Blockchain and DLT will grow whether you swear by Bitcoin or you scream that it has no fundamentals.

Hence, it is not necessary for you to invest in cryptocurrencies; you can simply sit on the bylines, learn about DLT slowly, and become a user if it does become mainstream.

If you do choose to go down the rabbit hole, I hope you find the adventure enriching. Remember, it is not about the end goal, but rather how you have grown because of the journey. You can make a lot of money, or you can lose it all, and then what?

At the end of the tunnel, you emerge a wiser person. Whatever it is, do not lose your sense of sanity and do not miss out on the present moments of life just because of an obsession with cryptocurrencies.

The decentralised future lies beyond the looking glass.

Live long and prosper.

Bibliography

Baumeister, F. Roy, and Brad J. Bushman. "Two Types Of Social Influence." *Social Psychology And Human Nature, 225–227*. Wadsworth: Cengage Learning, 2011.

Bernard, Zoe. "Everything you need to know about Bitcoin, its mysterious origins, and the many alleged identities of its creator," *Business Insider*, last modified December 2, 2017. https://www.businessinsider.com/bitcoin-history-cryptocurrency-satoshi-nakamoto-2017-12/?IR=T/#wait-so-who-is-this-japanese-american-guy-named-satoshi-nakamoto-7

Binance Team. "Summary of the Phishing and Attempted Stealing Incident on Binance," Binance, last modified March 8, 2018. https://support.binance.com/hc/en-us/articles/360001547431-Summary-of-the-Phishing-and-Attempted-Stealing-Incident-on-Binance

"Bitcoin price, charts, market cap, and other metrics," CoinMarketCap. Accessed August 11, 2018. https://coinmarketcap.com/currencies/bitcoin/#charts

Carlson, Ben. "How Framing Affects Investment Decisions & Outcomes," A Wealth Of Common Sense, last modified August 28, 2014. http://awealthofcommonsense.com/2014/08/framing-investment-decisions/

Carroll, Lewis. *Alice's Adventures in Wonderland*. Peterborough, Ont. :Broadview Press, 2000.

Choy, Wai and Pengtao Teng. "When Smart Contracts are Outsmarted: The Parity Wallet "Freeze" and Software Liability in the Internet of Value," Blockchain And The Law, last modified on December 22, 2017. https://www.blockchainandthelaw.com/2017/12/when-smart-contracts-are-outsmarted-the-parity-wallet-freeze-and-software-liability-in-the-internet-of-value/

Comin, Hobjin and others. "TECHNOLOGY DIFFUSION," Our World In Data, 2004, quoted in Jeff Desjardins, "A brief history of technology," World Economic Forum, last modified February 16, 2018. https://www.weforum.org/agenda/2018/02/the-rising-speed-of-technological-adoption

Curran, Brian. "What is The Tangle? Complete Guide to IOTA's Directed Acyclic Graph (DAG)," Blockonomi, last modified July 24, 2018. https://blockonomi.com/iota-tangle/

Cyrill, Melissa. "Bitcoin Market Unfazed by China Ban," *China* Briefing, last modified November 13, 2017. http://www.china-briefing.com/news/2017/11/13/cryptocurrency-market-unfazed-by-china-ban.html

Dixon, Julia. "The e-gold story," *DGC Magazine,* last modified June 27, 2013. http://dgcmagazine.com/the-e-gold-story/

Duca, John V. "Subprime Mortgage Crisis," Federal Reserve History, last modified November 22, 2013. https://www.federalreservehistory.org/essays/subprime_mortgage_crisis

Harrington, Lauren. "Security, Currency or Utility, How Do You Classify Your Cryptocurrency?" IntelligentHQ, last modified March 26, 2018. https://www.intelligenthq.com/resources/security-currency-utility-classify-cryptocurrency/

Investopedia staff. "Five Steps Of A Bubble," *Forbes,* last modified June 17, 2010. https://www.forbes.com/2010/06/17/guide-financial-bubbles-personal-finance-bubble.html#52e0a497af31

IOTA Foundation, "What is IOTA?" IOTA. Accessed August 29, 2018. https://www.iota.org/get-started/what-is-iota

Kelly, Gordon. "eBay Suffers Massive Security Breach, All Users Must Change Their Passwords," *Forbes,* last modified May 21, 2014. https://www.forbes.com/sites/gordonkelly/2014/05/21/ebay-suffers-massive-security-breach-all-users-must-their-change-passwords/#179274bf7492

Lord, Nate. "A TIMELINE OF THE ASHLEY MADISON HACK," *Digital Guardian,* last modified July 27, 2017. https://digitalguardian.com/blog/timeline-ashley-madison-hack

Madeira, Antonio. "The DAO, The Hack, The Soft Fork and The Hard Fork," Crypto Compare, last modified July 30, 2018. https://www.cryptocompare.com/coins/guides/the-dao-the-hack-the-soft-fork-and-the-hard-fork/

Martin, Felix. *Money: The Unauthorised Biography*. Bodley Head, 2013.

"Mass Media, Agenda Setting Theory," University of Twente, last modified February 27, 2017. https://www.utwente.nl/en/bms/communication-theories/sorted-by-cluster/Mass%20Media/Agenda-Setting_Theory/

McIntosh, Rachel. "Texan Regulator Orders Suspected 'Scamcoin' BitConnect to Cease and Desist," *Finance* Magnates, last modified January 5, 2018. https://www.financemagnates.com/

cryptocurrency/news/texan-regulator-orders-suspected-scamcoin-bitconnect-cease-desist/

Munro, Andrew. "Ethereum is not a security, tokens can change category SEC says," Finder AU, last modified June 15, 2018. https://www.finder.com.au/ethereum-is-not-a-security-tokens-can-change-category-sec-says

Nakamura, Yuji. "Coincheck to Repay Users Who Lost Money in $400 Million Hack," *Bloomberg,* last modified January 28, 2018. https://www.bloomberg.com/news/articles/2018-01-27/coincheck-to-repay-customers-who-lost-money-in-400-million-hack

Nakamoto, Satoshi. "Bitcoin: A Peer-to-Peer Electronic Cash System", bitcoin.org, last modified November 1, 2008. https://bitcoin.org/bitcoin.pdf

"Nearly Half of Americans Say Volatile Markets are an Easy Way to Make a Profit: AICPA Survey," AICPA, last modified August 9, 2018. https://www.aicpa.org/press/pressreleases/2018/americans-say-volatile-markets-are-easy-way-to-make-profit.html

Norry, Andrew. "The History of the Mt Gox Hack: Bitcoin's Biggest Heist," *Blockonomi,* last modified July 2, 2018. https://blockonomi.com/mt-gox-hack/

Nova, Annie. "Managing the stress of owning bitcoin and other cryptocurrencies," CNBC, last modified January 9, 2018. https://www.cnbc.com/2018/01/09/managing-the-stress-of-owning-bitcoin-and-other-cryptocurrencies.html

"Once a leader in virtual currencies, China turns against them." *The Economist*. Last modified September 30, 2017. https://www.economist.com/finance-and-economics/2017/09/30/once-a-leader-in-virtual-currencies-china-turns-against-them

Osborne, Charlie. "Verge blockchain comes under attack, again," ZDNet, last modified May 23, 2018. https://www.zdnet.com/article/verge-blockchain-comes-under-attack-again/

Quentson, Andrew. "Bitcoin Mining Pool Ghash.io DDos-ed in Response to threat of 51% attack?" CCN, last modified June 15, 2014. https://www.ccn.com/bitcoin-mining-pool-ghash-io-ddos-ed-response-51-attack/

Roberts, Daniel. "Here's your simple guide to the bitcoin halving," *Yahoo Finance,* last modified July 10, 2016. https://finance.yahoo.com/news/bitcoin-halving-blockchain-mining-000000868.html

Takeo, Yuko and Maiko Takahashi. "Crypto Investors Face Tax of Up to 55% in Japan," *Bloomberg,* last modified February 9, 2018. https://www.bloomberg.com/news/articles/2018-02-08/crypto-investors-in-japan-face-tax-of-up-to-55-on-their-takings

Weissman, Cale Guthrie. "Zuckerberg keeps insisting Facebook doesn't sell our data. What it does is even worse." *Fast* Company, last modified April 4, 2018. https://www.fastcompany.com/40554491/zuckerberg-keeps-insisting-facebook-doesnt-sell-our-data-what-it-does-is-even-worse

"What is ledger? definition and meaning." *BusinessDictionary*. Accessed August 11, 2018. http://www.businessdictionary.com/definition/ledger.html

Wieczner, Jen. "$1 Billion Bitcoins Lost in Mt. Gox Hack to Be Returned to Victims," *Fortune,* last modified June 22, 2018. http://fortune.com/2018/06/22/bitcoin-price-mt-gox-trustee/

Wong, Kristin. "The Many Different Types of Investments, and How They Work," *Life Hacker*, last modified February 5, 2015. https://twocents.lifehacker.com/the-many-different-types-of-investments-and-how-they-w-1683582510

About The Author

Having majored in Communications, and Psychology, I have been conditioned to be extremely inquisitive and critical of the things and happenings around me.

It was during my stint with an e-commerce startup when I first came across the concept of Smart Contracts (late 2016) and dived into Ethereum, and later on, cryptocurrencies. My approach in assessing startup companies and the feasibility of their businesses turned out to be really handy in helping me evaluate the many different cryptocurrencies.

Now that I have grasped most of the basic concepts about blockchain technology and entered long-term positions in my desired cryptocurrencies, my next step will be to work on short-term, daily trading and to experiment with other technical indicators. On the technology end, I will definitely be following closely on IOTA's Qubic and ARK's Smart Contracts.

Who knows, I just might write another book on technical trading. For now, follow me at www.herzigansel.com where I will document my trades and blog about the lessons learnt.

H. Ansel

Hansel, 2018

"I may just be a tiny drop of water. Give me the light, and I will paint your world in rainbows." — Hansel.

Copyright © 2018. Herzig Ansel.
All Rights Reserved.

www.ingramcontent.com/pod-product-compliance
Lightning Source LLC
Chambersburg PA
CBHW020431220526
45464CB00002B/654